The · Book · of

Beginnings

Creation

and the Promise

of Redemption

BEN CLAUSEN & GERALD WHEELER

REVIEW AND HERALD® PUBLISHING ASSOCIATION
HAGERSTOWN, MD 21740

Copyright © 2006 by
Review and Herald® Publishing Association
All rights reserved

The Review and Herald® Publishing Association publishes biblically based materials for
spiritual, physical, and mental growth and Christian discipleship.

The authors assume full responsibility for the accuracy of all facts and quotations as cited
in this book.

This book was
Edited by Gerald Wheeler
Copyedited by James Cavil
Cover design by Trent Truman
Cover image by Lars Justinen/Goodsalt.com
Electronic makeup by Shirley M. Bolivar
Typeset: Bembo 11/13

PRINTED IN U.S.A.

10 09 08 07 06   5 4 3 2 1

R&H Cataloging Service
The book of beginnings, by Ben Clausen and Gerald Wheeler.
    1. Bible. OT. Genesis—Study and teaching   I. Wheeler,
Gerald, 1943-   . II. Title.

                222.11

ISBN 10: 0-8280-1985-1
ISBN 13: 978-0-8280-1985-9

Dedication

To **Conrad,** *who first sparked my*
interest in science and origins questions.

To **Debbie,** *who helped me realize*
there is more to life than reason and argument.

To **Karen,** *who gave me reason for writing*
and who opened the doors to literature and philosophy.

~ ~ ~

To **Alexander,** *who, when asked at the age*
of 20 months what he was doing with
his Tinkertoys, would answer, "Making, making!"

**Other books
by
Gerald Wheeler:**
James White: Innovator and Overcomer

To order additional copies of
The Book of Beginnings,
by
Ben Clausen and Gerald Wheeler,
**call
1-800-765-6955.**

Visit us at
www.reviewandherald.com
for information on other Review and Herald® products.

Contents

Introduction

As a trained scientist, Ben Clausen wrote chapters 1 through 6 exploring the various scientific and practical issues of the biblical account of origins in Genesis 1-11. Gerald Wheeler authored chapters 7 through 13 and the Theological Perspective inserts in chapters 1 through 6.

1

"In the Beginning"

Genesis 1

My daughter and I craned our necks to see what the United Nations has called the greatest artistic masterpiece of all time—the frescoed ceiling of the Sistine Chapel. One need only see a reproduction of the two hands, or just the fingertips, to recognize Michelangelo's famous painting *The Creation of Adam*. It, however, is only one of the nine panels that cover the ceiling. What did Michelangelo choose as his theme? Stories from the first 11 chapters of Genesis.

The first scene portrays God emerging from the chaos and creating light—He Himself forming the line dividing light from darkness. In the second panel the Almighty touches into existence the sun and moon as one angel shields their eyes from the dazzling sun while another cloaks their head for warmth near the cold moon. The next scene shows God poised over the oceans, dividing land from water. In the fourth panel God's strong hand infuses life into Adam as the deity contemplates him with love. Here Michelangelo portrayed the Eternal with an old face and flowing white hair, but a powerful young body. The central scene depicts Eve, as if drawn by God from Adam's side, expressing gratitude to her Maker.

Following the central scene, evil intrudes itself as a tempter from whom Eve takes the forbidden fruit. The faces of the pair become disfigured by sin, and Eve cringes in dread behind her husband. In the Flood portrayal despairing people try to save themselves in a futile attempt to reach high ground. The square ark in the background looks like a temple or sanctuary. Then, in the final sad scene, old Noah sprawls on the ground, drunk and naked, as Ham points at him contemptuously. Shem restrains and reproves his brother, while Japheth covers his father with a piece of clothing, at the same time averting his eyes.[1]

Genesis, the story of beginnings, addresses all the fundamental issues of existence. It sets the stage for everything we know: God, the natural universe, humanity, and the existence of good and evil. This biblical book lays the foundation for all the questions asked by philosophy about knowledge, ultimate meaning, free will, the soul, ethics, happiness, and success. The rest of the Bible frequently alludes to Genesis 1-11 in discussing atonement, judgment, resurrection, and final restoration.[2] And it is all told as a story, the most easily understood yet most profound way of communicating insights. It is a narrative that had meaning for the ancient Hebrew culture as well as having significance for today's modern scientific mind-set. Because it speaks to fundamental human issues, it has lasted.

As we study the story of beginnings in the next few chapters, we will attempt a balanced presentation, laying out a range of data along with various possible interpretations. These chapters provide a summary of topics in Genesis 1-11 and emphasize their wide-ranging importance, for space does not permit us to go into depth on any particular topic.★

Everyone has a bias as they study, so I will try to outline mine here. I come to the topics in this book as a scientist who looks at nature as marred by sin and interprets it through finite human senses and reasoning. I take science seriously as saying something about reality, but do not regard it as the final word on every subject. I also approach these topics as a Christian trusting Christ as Lord and accepting Scripture as God's Word written and interpreted by humans. I accept God's Word as authoritative, but emphasize that when using such an approach I am not engaging in science. I do not believe that the Bible presents the best scientific model for origins or even a scientific model, for Scripture presents much more than a naturalistic model, much more than a model based only on what can be perceived by the physical senses.

Thus our explorations will not provide the one and only right answer, but they will provide clues and suggestions to help our understanding. I come with many questions myself, but belief is possible in spite of uncertainty. The Seventh-day Adventist position has its share of problems, but for me it is better than the alternatives.

Finally, it is well to remember that people are more important than facts, doctrines, or being "right." Christ rarely tried to prove His point.[3] Signs and evidence were not useful.[4] While Christ did not compromise with error,[5] He did avoid controversy,[6] as we are also to do.[7] He spoke to the heart more than to the reason.[8]

Although it is fun to speculate about the details (and we will do some of that), it will not be the main emphasis. It is easy to get lost in "trifling distinctions" and miss "the living realities"[9] and weightier matters (Matt. 23:23, NKJV). Looking at the broader picture has a precedent in the way that Jesus broadened the Jews' understanding of the Messiah's work and role. Although they feared He was abolishing the law, He was in fact fulfilling it (Matt. 5:17).

The following two sections outline the importance of origins-related issues for me personally and for generally understanding the great controversy about God's character. The next two sections will aid in understanding scriptural references to natural phenomena by putting them in the context of other ancient Near Eastern origins stories, as well as in terms of a modern scientific culture. The final section outlines modern science's own story of origins with its roots in the Judeo-Christian worldview of nature, and how scientists have found compatibility of science with Christian beliefs.

Important Issues

The issues addressed in Genesis 1-11 were ones vital to me as I grew up.

God: As a preacher's kid, I attended evangelistic meetings, studied Bible correspondence courses, competed successfully in Bible contests, read through the Conflict of the Ages Series, went as a student missionary to Zimbabwe, and attended only Seventh-day Adventist schools up through part of my graduate work.

The Natural World: At the same time, God's second book of nature fascinated me. I collected butterflies, assembled a radio and electronic lab kit, and hiked the Appalachian Mountains. The first book I read by myself was a Christmas present from my sister in second grade—a children's book on Albert Einstein. The best part of the year was family vacations in the Rocky Mountains.

People: I had a high regard for both the inspired record and the natural world. Facts from both areas took precedence over people relationships. Thus it only gradually dawned on me, a natural-born geek, that people are more important than facts and logic.

Evil: The horrors of evil struck me with full force on my first trip to Russia. To reach the Dubna nuclear facility on the Volga River 60 miles north of Moscow, we drove along the Moscow-Volga Canal. Political prisoners using shovels and wheelbarrows had dug it during the Stalinist regime. Speaking of the Gulag, Solzhenitsyn says, "Stalin simply needed a great construction project *somewhere* which would devour many working hands and many lives . . . with the reliability of a gas execution van but more cheaply."[10]

The book of Genesis introduces God, people, the natural world, evil, and their various relations in time. Genesis 1-11 describes a God who intervenes in the natural world, in human affairs, and in our personal lives. Seventh-day Adventists place a particular emphasis on time because the seventh-day Sabbath memorializes a recent past creation and prophecy points to the soon future Advent.

The world needs people "who will stand for the right though the heavens fall."[11] Some issues in Genesis 1-11 require us to take such positions, whereas others are peripheral. Many earth history details may not be so crucial, and many historic or scientific details in Genesis 1-11 are not worth arguing about. Details and symbols can easily become as meaningless for us today as sacrifices and rules were for people in Christ's day.

I find it more useful to emphasize the Bible's great controversy story and the integral part that Genesis 1-11 plays in it. Ancient Zoroastrianism, Milton's *Paradise Lost,* and other sources have had a sense for this story, but none quite like the great literature of the Bible.[12] The major issues concern God's character, and our trust in Him over our own wisdom.

God's Character

Rational and Dependable. Scripture portrays God as dependable and as the giver of stable natural and moral laws for His creation. Because He created us in His image, we are rational beings. Alvin Plantinga, a well-known Christian philosopher, suggests that minds created by God would be geared toward discovering truth, whereas a naturalistic worldview offers no reason to believe that human thinking would ever be reliable.*

God thus provides evidence for belief, although not compelling proof, because He also gives freedom of choice. Likewise, Christians would do well to "be ready always to give an answer to every man that asketh you a reason" (1 Peter 3:15, KJV), but not to demand absolute proof. Unfortunately, Eve based her decision only on sense perception and reason (Gen. 3:6). This leads to the next set of divine attributes.

Omnipotent, Omniscient, and Eternal. Human reason is important, but has its limits. God is much greater than human reason can understand or imagine from studying either nature or Scripture (Isa. 55:8). The book of Job talks much about God's wisdom (e.g., Job 28) and the wonders of creation as well as the finiteness of human understanding (Job 38:2, 3) and its limited ability to answer questions about nature or anything else (Job 40:4; 42:2, 3).

Humanity's concepts about God are too small.★ The second commandment warns against worshipping any incomplete human representation or understanding of what the true God is like. The Israelites had not seen God, so were to make no representation of Him (Deut. 4:15-19), lest they come to believe that the true God was no greater than what they used to depict Him with.

Truthful and Just. The Scriptures provide a true record of God's just dealings with humanity and present all the data, including the discouragement of Lamentations, the sex and violence of Judges, and the pleasures of sin in Egypt. "Truth can afford to be fair. No true doctrine will lose anything by close investigation."[13]

We can also find truth in the natural world. Honesty with data from the natural world means looking at all of it. As we shall see, arguments for creation as well as evolution have their problems.[14]

Speaking of objective truth, atheist physicist Steven Weinberg[15] observes that in one sense religious conservatives are closer to scientists than religious liberals. Conservatives "believe in what they believe because it is true," whereas liberals "think that different people can believe in different mutually exclusive things without any of them being wrong."

However, he goes on to add that "it is conservative dogmatic religion that does the harm" with its "long cruel story of crusade and jihad and inquisition and pogrom." Inspiration agrees: "A jealous regard for what is termed theological truth often accompanies a hatred of genuine truth as made manifest in life. The darkest chapters of history are burdened with the record of crimes committed by bigoted religionists."[16]

Weinberg would like to strike a balance between the contributions of religion and its problems, but in so doing he believes that "it is not safe to assume that religious persecution and holy wars are perversions of true religion." However, I believe that bigotry, arrogance, dishonesty, and sloppy science *are* a perversion of true Christianity. This leads to the next set of attributes for God.

Loving and Merciful. The personal God of Scripture is a deity of love and mercy. We are the result of choice by a loving God, not the outcome of accident or blind chance. Thus we have meaning and purpose in life. Yet the world we know is not a perfect one. It is flawed and often dangerous. Few would deny that it is permeated with what we can only call evil. So how does one deal with the problem of evil? "I have to admit that sometimes nature seems more beautiful than strictly necessary," Weinberg comments. "It is almost irresistible to imagine that all this beauty was somehow laid on for our benefit. But the God of birds and trees would have to be also the God of birth defects and cancer." [17]

Christ partially answered the question when He declared, "An enemy has done this" (Matt. 13:28, NKJV). However, even this is not sufficient. "No intangible principle, no impersonal essence or mere abstraction, can satisfy the needs and longings of human beings in this life of struggle with sin and sorrow and pain. It is not enough to believe in law and force. . . . We need to clasp a hand that is warm, to trust in a heart full of tenderness." [18]

How then does one portray God's character and actions within any particular cultural setting—the supernatural in human terms? Paul heard "unspeakable words" in vision (2 Cor. 12:4, KJV) and recognized that we have no concept of what God is preparing for us (1 Cor. 2:9). Daniel and John had a similar problem in the their apocalyptic books. The people in Christ's day witnessed a literal Advent, but it was far from what they had pictured. Describing divine things in human language can be like making idols—it limits our perception. God and reality are more than can be imagined, not less, for Bible descriptions can be correct without being complete. Thus God communicated to us through stories—descriptions that we cannot analyze scientifically, for science explains the universe in purely human, concrete terms.

Since we all want explanations of why things are the way we see them today, we trace the effects of today back to the causes of yesterday. Different cultures portray the history of beginnings through such devices as story, epic, saga, myth, metanarrative, or scientific model.

Ancient Near Eastern Stories

Creation accounts from Mesopotamia, Egypt, and Greece often parallel the stories of the Bible. As we briefly describe some of these narratives, notice the similarities to, but also the differences from, the Genesis record. Also, consider possible explanations for the similarities: a common source, borrowing, or an attempt to reach a specific culture (God's people shared much with the culture around them).

In one of the earliest Mesopotamian epics, Gilgamesh★ starts as a bad king. His subjects ask the gods for help, and one of them creates the wild man, Enkidu, who eventually becomes friends with Gilgamesh. Enkidu loses his strength and wildness to a harlot, but gains knowledge and civilization. After Enkidu dies, Gilgamesh realizes that he too will die, so he searches for eternal life. During his pilgrimage he enters a brilliant garden of gems, in which every tree bears precious stones. Later a man named Utnapishtim tells him a story of a flood so great that it frightened even the gods. To save Utnapishtim, one god instructed him to build a boat. After the flood the man opens a window in the boat, the craft comes to rest on a mountain, the gods smell the odor of a sacrifice, and he and his wife are blessed by the gods and made immortal. Utnapishtim offers Gilgamesh a secret plant that will make him young again, but before Gilgamesh can use it, a snake eats it. Eventually Gilgamesh accepts death.

In the Akkadian Epic of Atrahasis,★ Enlil, god of the earth, puts the other gods to work digging the Tigris and Euphrates rivers. When the gods tire, Enki, god of the deep, suggests that they create man from clay and blood to do their work. The noise of the growing human population keeps Enlil awake at night, so the enraged deity sends a seven-day flood to annihilate all humanity. Enki warns a man named Atrahasis to build a large boat and load it with animals. Afterward, the gods become hungry for offerings, so Atrahasis prepares a sacrifice.

A later Babylon work, the Enuma Elish,★ features Tiamat and Marduk. Tiamat is the chaos monster, goddess of the sea. Marduk, the patron god of Babylon, kills Tiamat and divides the corpse, using half for the earth and half for the sky, complete with bars to keep the chaotic waters from escaping. Then he sets up the celestial luminaries to establish days, months, and seasons. A god is killed to provide blood and bone for the creation of human beings, who are to perform menial tasks. The gods then rest and praise Marduk for his greatness.

The Egyptian creation myths★ picture a swirling watery chaos. In one myth the sun god (Atum) and a dry mound (Ma'at) emerge from the water. Atum, the "Great He-She" creator, mates with his shadow, producing two other gods, one of which represents the "principles of order" and the other the "principle of Life." When Atum weeps, tears hit the ground and grow into men, for whom Atum creates a world. More gods then come into being. Egyptian artists pictured a sky goddess as the heavens, separated from the earth god by the goddess of the air. In the Memphis version of creation a god named Ptah seems to precede all these gods as the self-created one, who created all other gods by his heart and used his tongue to give them breath.

Greek mythology★ has the first gods emerging from chaos, the primeval nothingness. One of the gods, Prometheus ("foresight"), creates the first people. He acts as a mediator between humanity and the gods, eventually stealing fire for humans from the powerful god Zeus. The enraged Zeus has Prometheus bound to a stake, and to punish mankind, Zeus orders the gods to create the first woman. They fashion her body from clay, and the various gods give gifts to Pandora ("all gifts"), including a box that she is never to open. Mankind has been living in Paradise, but one day Pandora opens the box, releasing old age, disease, hard work, and crime on the entire human race. The world is hopeless until Pandora once again opens the box, and Hope appears. Later Zeus determines to destroy human wickedness by a great deluge. Prometheus' son builds an ark and provisions it. After nine days of flooding, the vessel touches solid ground; he and his wife are the only surviving humans.

Many other cultures have stories of beginnings,* but these examples are sufficient to show the themes, metaphors, and symbolism in common with Genesis, such as watery chaos, the making of the sun and moon, sky, and dry land, as well as a first man and woman, a garden, a trickster serpent, evil, death and immortality, sacrifice, and a deluge. The biblical writers expressed God's story in familiar words and images, just as missionaries do when working in different cultures. Genesis, however, uses these themes to assert its own monotheistic theology. The Genesis story is unique in depicting a single, all-powerful, unselfish God distinct from His creation that He brings out of nothing simply by the power of His word in history.

Most ancient cultures viewed the world as endless, repeating a series of cycles, usually seasonal in nature. But the Bible depicts a different worldview. God's actions are part of a linear concept of history, one that is going somewhere—with a beginning and an end. "Genuine historical consciousness had its birth among the Hebrews" because of their "perception of the purposefulness of history."[19] The Ten Commandments begin with a historical statement "I am the Lord your God, who brought you out of the land of Egypt" (Ex. 20:2, NKJV). This concept flows into the historical character of the Christian faith: "the Word became flesh" (John 1:14, NKJV), an event witnessed by humans (Luke 1:2; 1 John 1:1).

When the Bible Talks About Nature

The major Bible themes come through strong and clear, but as they say, "the devil is in the details." How should we understand the language details of Genesis in today's scientific culture? Following are several possible nonexclusive ways of interpreting such references.

1. Literary works use metaphor and simile. Bible examples might in-

clude: the sea shut behind doors or bars (Job 38:8-11), a storehouse for the snow, rain, hail, and wind (Job 38:22; Ps. 135:7; Jer. 10:13; 51:16), corners of the earth (Isa. 11:12; Rev. 7:1), and a solid "dome" of heaven with windows that can be opened (Gen. 7:11; 8:2; Isa. 64:1; Eze. 1:1; Mal. 3:10; Mark 1:10; Acts 7:56; Rev. 19:11).

2. Language of appearance describes natural phenomena in terms of what they resemble or remind one of. We today still talk of the sun rising and setting, while recognizing that the earth actually spins on its axis. The Bible speaks of the earth as stationary on fixed foundations or pillars and the sun as moving or changing its movement.[20]

3. The Bible intended its descriptions for the average person, not scientists who require precisely defined terminology. Such descriptions might include rabbits chewing the cud (Deut. 14:7),* a grain of wheat dying in the ground (John 12:24), salt losing its savor (Matt. 5:13), insects with four legs (Lev. 11:21, 22), or the Temple's laver with a circumference/diameter ratio of 3 rather than π (3.14) (2 Chron. 4:2). Examples from Ellen White's writings include falling stars and stars in our solar system[21] and a thousand worlds lighted by our own sun.[22]

4. The biblical authors did not bother to correct every cultural misunderstanding, such as the idea of being "smitten by the moon" (see Ps. 121:6),[23] the parable of the rich man and Lazarus (Luke 16:19-31),[24] or "light in the eyes" (see Matt. 6:22). However, God did later correct one erroneous concept Jacob had about animal breeding (Gen. 30:37-42; 31:10-12). A recent research study emphasizes the inspired nature of Ellen White's writings, but notes that she at times used the then-current understandings that may not necessarily be the same as the medical explanations used today.[25] If she had used a nonstandard explanation in the inspired writings, many might have questioned their validity. This suggests caution in trying to derive modern scientific details from the Bible's language.

5. Some biblical details about nature otherwise unknown by ancient cultures have since been confirmed, such as the stars in the Pleiades being bound together (Job 38:31).[26] Historical research has shown that the ancient king chronologies do add up correctly.[27]

To summarize: "The Bible, perfect as it is in its simplicity, does not answer to the great ideas of God, for infinite ideas cannot be perfectly embodied in finite vehicles of thought."[28]

Science Developed in a Christian Culture

Just as with other cultures, today's world has its explanation of beginnings.

Modern scientific culture trusts evolution as "the creation myth of our age."[29] It includes the concept of a big bang, stellar evolution, matter accreting to form the earth, plate tectonics, and life's progression. The goal of science is to organize empirically derived data from the natural world and make sense out of it using natural law and reason. Just as Seventh-day Adventists like the great controversy metanarrative because it fits many individual pieces of revelation into an overall cohesive picture, even so scientists like the long-age paradigm because it puts so many pieces of empirical data into an overall explanatory story.

This conflict between scientific and religious paradigms became forcefully apparent to me one summer when my brother needed to attend meetings on creation and evolution. Our whole family spent our vacation in the area to be with him. I attended most of the science/religion meetings and was especially impressed with the emotional involvement (at times anger) of some of the participants. How do we deal with the conflict?

Science From Christianity. The science-religion conflict scenario is only of recent origin. Historians of science have suggested that the Judeo-Christian environment of Western Europe and belief in a monotheistic God were responsible for the development of modern science in that culture. A number of factors encourage the acceptance of modern science.

First of all, the Judeo-Christian God is a *lawgiver.* His creation would then be understandable, predictable, and amenable to study with rational inquiry. In contrast, the polytheistic warring factions and arbitrary gods of other cultures would make a world in which rational inquiry would be useless.

The *personal* God of Christianity is separate from nature, thus making abstract laws for nature reasonable. In contrast, a belief in impersonal nature gods makes experimentation on nature a fearful and forbidden endeavor.

Genesis depicts God *creating a good world* worthy of human study, so that one learns about nature from nature itself, not from some authority. In contrast, the Greeks tried to understand nature through philosophy, so experimentation was a low priority. They believed that the real world was only an imperfect representation of the ideal, one that might quite likely give erroneous results if actually studied.

God created *humanity in His image.* As a result, human beings would share at least some of His rationality and ability to understand the world around them. The Lord made human beings stewards of the world and gave them dominion over it. Thus they would need to learn how to control it.

Scientists as Christians. It is possible to be both a productive scientist and a person of faith. In fact, most of the founders of science were individuals of faith.

A Theological Perspective of the Biblical Story of Origins

From its very first verses Genesis introduces a theme that will continue throughout the rest of the Bible: God's creatorship. His creatorship has three aspects. He creates:

(1) physical matter and life;
(2) a special people;
(3) history.

Most people recognize the first aspect. God made our world and all the forms of life on it. The second aspect is less well known. God not only created the first human couple; He brought into being a special people for Himself—and continues to create a people in the last days. But the third aspect is the least familiar even to many Christians.

The Bible declares that God is the maker of not only heaven and earth but also the events that occur in them, especially those things that fulfill the plan of salvation. God brought the physical world into existence and rested from that part of His creative role. But humanity rebelled when Adam and Eve ate from the forbidden tree. Instead of abandoning them, however, He told the serpent that Someone "will strike your head" (Gen. 3:15). The Lord would fulfill that promise through the historical events that He initiated for our salvation. The Bible is the story of His role as creator of history. God can intervene in His creation.

Isaiah 40:18-20 dismisses idols as nothing more than human-made objects. But God has existed from the beginning, and He not only created the physical universe, including the earth, but also controls events in our world (verses 22-24). Things can happen only if He permits them. "To whom then will you compare me, or who is my equal? says the Holy One" (verse 25). The Lord answers His own question by pointing to His creative power. "Lift up your eyes on high and see: Who created these?" (verse 26). "The Lord is the everlasting God, the Creator of the ends of the earth" (verse 28). The true and one and only God is the creator of all that is, including human history.

Notice how intimately Scripture links both physical creation and the creation of history. "It is he who sits above the circle of the earth . . . ; who stretches out the heavens like a curtain, and spreads them like a tent to live in; who brings princes to naught, and makes the rulers of earth as nothing" (Isa. 40:22, 23). Here God ties His creative powers with His ability to control political and other events. God uses His creative power to bring about events that will restore His sin-damaged creation.

* For those who wish to explore some topics in greater depth, an accompanying Web site (http://www.grisda.org/genesis/) provides additional resources, especially for topics marked with a star.

[1] Enrico Bruschini, *Masterpieces of the Vatican* (London: Scala Publishers, 2004), pp. 102, 107-122.
[2] Adam and Eve (Mark 10:6; 1 Cor. 15:22, 45; 2 Cor. 11:3; 1 Tim. 2:13, 14); Cain and Abel (Heb. 11:4); Enoch (Jude 14); Noah (Matt. 24:37, 38; Luke 17:26, 27; Heb. 11:7; 1 Peter 3:20; 2 Peter 2:5; 3:5, 6). See also John T. Baldwin, ed., *Creation, Catastrophe, and*

Calvary (Hagerstown, Md.: Review and Herald Pub. Assn., 2000).

[3] Ellen G. White, *The Desire of Ages* (Mountain View, Calif.: Pacific Press Pub. Assn., 1898), pp. 119, 465.

[4] *Ibid.,* pp. 164, 198, 406, 408, 799.

[5] *Ibid.,* pp. 355, 356.

[6] *Ibid.,* pp. 85, 89, 119, 175, 188, 253, 350, 396, 450, 497, 498.

[7] *Ibid.,* pp. 181, 434.

[8] *Ibid.,* pp. 142, 151, 455.

[9] *Ibid.,* p. 396.

[10] Aleksandr I. Solzhenitsyn, *The Gulag Archipelago: 1918-1956* (New York: Harper & Row, 1975), vol. 3, p. 86.

[11] Ellen G. White, *Education* (Mountain View, Calif.: Pacific Press Pub. Assn., 1903), p. 57.

[12] *Ibid.,* p. 159; White, *Counsels to Parents, Teachers, and Students* (Mountain View, Calif.: Pacific Press Pub. Assn., 1913), pp. 428, 429.

[13] White, *Counsels to Writers and Editors* (Washington, D.C.: Review and Herald Pub. Assn., 1946), p. 35.

[14] Del Ratzsch, *The Battle of Beginnings: Why Neither Side Is Winning the Creation-Evolution Debate* (Downers Grove, Ill.: InterVarsity Press, 1996), p. 310.

[15] Steven Weinberg, *Dreams of a Final Theory* (New York: Vintage Books, 1992), pp. 257, 258.

[16] White, *The Desire of Ages,* p. 209.

[17] Weinberg, p. 250.

[18] White, *Education,* p. 133.

[19] John F. Priest, "Myth and Dream in Hebrew Scripture," in Joseph Campbell, ed., *Myths, Dreams, and Religion* (Dallas: Spring Pub., 1970), p. 53.

[20] A stationary earth (1 Sam. 2:8; 1 Chron. 16:30; Job 9:6; 26:11; 38:4, 6; Ps. 75:3; 93:1; 104:5; 119:90; Prov. 8:29) and a moving sun (Joshua 10:12, 13; Eccl. 1:5; Isa. 38:8; Hab. 3:11).

[21] White, *Education,* p. 14; *The Desire of Ages,* p. 465.

[22] White, *The Desire of Ages,* p. 21.

[23] George W. Reid, "Smitten by the Moon?" *Adventist Review,* Apr. 28, 1983, p. 7.

[24] Ellen G. White, *Christ's Object Lessons* (Washington, D.C.: Review and Herald Pub. Assn., 1941), p. 263.

[25] Don S. McMahon, *Acquired or Inspired? Exploring the Origins of the Adventist Lifestyle* (Victoria, Australia: Signs Pub. Co., 2005), pp. 29-34.

[26] Theodore P. Snow, *Essentials of the Dynamic Universe: An Introduction to Astronomy* (Minneapolis: West Pub. Co., 1991), p. 319.

[27] Edwin R. Thiele, *The Mysterious Numbers of the Hebrew Kings: A Reconstruction of the Chronology of the Kingdoms of Israel and Judah,* rev. ed. (Grand Rapids: W. B. Eerdmans Pub. Co., 1965).

[28] Ellen G. White, *Selected Messages* (Washington, D.C.: Review and Herald Pub. Assn., 1958), book 1, p. 22.

[29] Mary Midgley, "Evolution as a Religion: A Comparison of Prophecies," *Zygon* 22, no. 2 (June 1987): 179.

2

"Let There Be . . ."
Genesis 1

Soon after we married, my wife and I went hiking at Arches National Park in Utah. In this desert area the trail is often difficult to locate, and Debbie worried about getting lost. Soon, though, we noticed heaps of rocks stacked on top of each other every 100 feet or so. These piles, known as cairns, appeared to be designed by intelligent humans, and we took them to represent trail markers. We used them to find the arches . . . and the way back to the trailhead.

The natural world exhibits similar evidence of intelligent design suggesting the existence of a Designer (Ps. 19:1; Rom. 1:20). William Paley, in his 1802 classic, *Natural Theology: or, Evidences of the Existence and Attributes of the Deity, Collected From the Appearances of Nature,* gave the example of finding a watch while walking in a field. Although one might infer that a rock in a field formed by natural processes and appeared there by chance, no one would conclude that about the watch. The Oxford atheist Richard Dawkins wrote a recent book entitled *The Blind Watchmaker* to refute evidence for intelligent design in nature, but even he recognizes evidence of design. On the first page he stated, "Biology is the study of complicated things that give the appearance of having been designed for a purpose."

Creation of the Physical Universe

God's first creative acts prepared the physical universe for life. He created simply by the power of His word (Ps. 33:6; Heb. 1:3; 11:3) and brought order out of chaos.

Light, the first and fundamental creation, is one of the most enigmatic of physical phenomena, since it paradoxically behaves as both a wave and a particle. As a wave light can be refracted, or bent, as it passes through a pair of glasses or a microscope lens. It displays interference patterns, as seen in the colors of a peacock wing or the hologram on a credit card. Beyond the visible light spectrum of red, orange, yellow, green, blue, and violet are sunburn-causing ultraviolet and the even more energetic X-rays. Below red we find infrared—felt as heat—microwaves used in ovens, and radio and TV waves. In addition, light sets the speed limit for the universe at 186,000 miles per second. According to the theory of special relativity, this speed is a constant and everything else is relative. This high speed is the "c" in Einstein's famous equation $E = mc^2$. When the mass "m" of a minute atom gets multiplied twice by the speed of light, the resulting energy gives us the atomic bomb.★

Besides light and other forms of energy, the universe consists of matter. The earth's fluid covering of air and water, for example, make life possible. The 20 percent oxygen and 80 percent nitrogen of the earth's atmosphere comprises an ideal mix of gases. More oxygen would make fire control difficult, whereas less oxygen would be insufficient for human life. Water covers 70 percent of the planet and makes up more than half of the composition of our bodies. Its ability to hold large amounts of heat decreases earth's temperature fluctuations to a range acceptable for life. Unlike most substances, water expands on freezing, with the result that ice floats; otherwise the ocean basins would freeze from the bottom up. Water is as important for chemistry and biology as light is for physics.★

The earth has the right properties for life.[1] Its speed of rotation is rapid enough to give an equitable climate over much of the earth, but not so fast as to cause a merry-go-round effect. The force of gravity of a much larger planet would be too great for humans to withstand. A smaller earth with less gravitational attraction would not be able to hold on to an atmosphere.

The earth's orbit is nearly circular, resulting in a constant distance from the sun and thus uniform heating for the earth's surface. The sun is the right distance from the earth to provide the necessary light, but not too much heat, thus allowing water to exist in abundance as a liquid. The moon provides strong enough tides to keep the oceans from stagnation, but not so powerful as to inundate the land areas.

This universe that God created and controls (Isa. 40:26) includes stars like our sun that are fueled by nuclear fusion, red giants so big they would engulf the orbit of Mercury, exploding supernovae resulting in temperatures of a billion degrees, neutron stars so dense that the mass of the earth would fit inside the Washington, D.C., Beltway, and black holes from which light never escapes.

The characteristics of the universe appear finely tuned for life. For example, the nuclei of most atoms contain many positively charged protons. Like electrical charges repel each other, so what makes all these protons stick together? Apparently it is some force stronger than the electric force, and for want of a better term, physicists call it the "strong force." To get the range of elements necessary for life, the ratio between these two forces must be carefully balanced. If the electric/strong force ratio were larger, protons would not be able to clump together. No heavier elements necessary for life, such as carbon and oxygen, would be stable. But if the ratio was smaller, protons would too easily clump together to form the heavy elements, leaving no single-proton hydrogen a constituent of water necessary for life. There might be plenty of gold and platinum, but no one would exist to enjoy them.

Speaking of our fine-tuned universe, Nobel prize winner Arno Penzias says that the universe has "the very delicate balance needed to provide exactly the conditions required to permit life, and one which has an underlying (one might say 'supernatural') plan."[2]

Creation of Life

Perhaps the most difficult natural feature of the universe to explain mechanistically is the existence of life. Sir Fred Hoyle compared the chance emergence of a simple cell to the likelihood that a tornado sweeping through a junkyard might fully assemble the scattered bits and pieces of a Boeing 747 found there.[3] Even a simple cell is extremely complex and adaptable. The amoeba, for example, is able to move, seek for and surround its food, respond to light and darkness, and reproduce.

A 2005 New Scientist article listed some of life's greatest "inventions," including photosynthesis, the eye, the brain, sex, colonial organisms (e.g., bees and ants), and symbiosis.[4] With symbiosis, not only is one organism adapted to its environment, but two organisms are adapted to each other. Thus birds eat the leeches they find between the teeth of crocodiles. Angler fish living in the black depths of the ocean have an appendage suspended in front of their mouths as a lure that hosts light-producing bacteria to attract prey. Leafcutter ants fertilize fungus with chopped-up leaves, and the fungus provides food for the ants.

The marvels of life on earth are endless. Our world's plants range from those in a mangrove swamp to those able to live in a dry desert, and from the mighty coast redwoods more than 300 feet tall to the long-lived bristlecone pine with thousands of rings. These organisms use the complex photosynthetic process to make their own food from light energy. Adaptations for reproduction include precise cooperation between plant and insect for pollination and a wide range of methods for seed dispersal: winged maple seeds, dandelion and cottonwood parachutes, explosive touch-me-not seeds, burdock stickers, and floating coconuts.

Birds are uniquely designed for flight, with hollow bones, breast muscles that form up to one third of total body weight, feathers that they can individually adjust, and a flow-through respiratory system. In size birds range from the 0.05-ounce hummingbird that can beat its wings at 200 beats per second up to the nine-foot-tall, 300-pound ostrich that can travel 30 miles per hour and has a 23-foot stride. The redheaded woodpecker hits the bark of a tree at a speed of up to 13 miles per hour for a deceleration of 10 g's. The common swift is airborne for two to four years, during which it sleeps, drinks, eats, and mates for a nonstop flight of as much as 300,000 miles. The arctic tern breeds north of the Arctic Circle and migrates to the Antarctic each year for a round trip of more than 20,000 miles.*

Land animals range from a shrew the size of a thumb to the seven-ton elephant. Prairie dog colonies in the southwestern United States have been known to cover more than 20,000 square miles and contain hundreds of millions of individuals.

The human body is fearfully and wonderfully made (Ps. 139:14). While taking biology classes in high school, I remember being amazed at the intricacies of the human body: the design of the red blood cell to carry oxygen; the immune and blood-clotting systems; the way electrochemical impulses travel along the nerves; the complexity of the eye; and the various hormones the body uses to regulate itself.

Until the eighteenth century people considered life to be the product of supernatural activity. Carolus Linnaeus, the father of taxonomy, instituted the binomial (two-word) nomenclature still used today to define genera and species. He developed his system as a product of his search for the distinct "kinds" of created organisms mentioned in Genesis.[5]

Biological Change. Humans desire both continuity and novelty in life, just as they like both cyclical sameness and linear change in the passage of time. During the nineteenth century Western society especially exhibited evidence of change, growth in knowledge, and technological progress. Charles Darwin proposed that change and progress occurred in the biological realm as well. He rejected the idea of fixity of species, the creationist view of the time that organisms never change or adapt to the environment. As evidence for change, he cited the various types of finches living on the Galapagos Islands (His observations were reasonable); we today can easily see the great variety of dogs. His theory of evolution was an extrapolation of the widespread variation he saw in tropical animals.

The fact that organisms change with time is now impossible to deny. The order in the fossil record appears to provide significant support for evolution, giving evidence of both large- and small-scale changes. Some similarities between organisms seem to be more easily explainable by common ancestry than by common design.

On the other hand, the amount of biological variation and change seems to have limits. And we have little direct evidence for the development of new basic types of organisms. Instead, new and complex organisms often appear suddenly rather than gradually in the geologic record. Few organisms with characteristics intermediate between major groups occur either among living animals or in the fossil record.[6] The current naturalistic explanation for origins doesn't seem compelling. Such scientific data provide clues about origins, but no proofs.

The Creation and Progression of Time

Genesis starts with a time statement, "In the beginning God" (Gen. 1:1, KJV), with its counterpart in John, "In the beginning was the Word" (John 1:1; see also Col. 1:16, 17). One third of the creative activity in Genesis 1 relates directly to time: the evening and morning set off the first day, and the heavenly bodies mark out the days, seasons, and years after the fourth day. On the other days God produces plants, sea creatures, birds, and animals much faster than anything we see today.

The interesting features of nature are those that change with time: the physical motion of bodies or waves, chemical reactions, biological change and evolution, and geological rates—all part of a dynamic universe and human activity. We want action! Linear time has a beginning, an end, and a sometimes complicated rate in between. Trying to understand how God relates to time and what happens when He intervenes in nature is even more challenging.

Beginnings for Time. At the beginning of the twentieth century Einstein and others envisioned an eternal static universe. Since everything in the universe attracts everything else by gravity, Einstein put an unknown repulsive force into his equations to explain why the universe doesn't collapse. Once the astronomer Hubble found evidence for an expanding universe, Einstein's repulsive force no longer seemed necessary, and he said this cosmological constant was the biggest mistake of his life. The universe isn't collapsing because it started off with a "big bang" that caused it to expand. For a while scientists resisted this concept of a beginning—it would require a Beginner, an effect without a cause, a limit to what science could explore. To paraphrase the concluding paragraphs of Robert Jastrow's *God and the Astronomers:* As scientists explored further and further back in time, they were about to conquer the mountain of knowledge, but quite unexpectedly found that theologians knew the ultimate answer all along. God had started things off.

Directionality of Time. The second law of thermodynamics requires a beginning for time and linear or historical directionality afterward. The second law puts into words the universally observed tendency toward increasing disorder, as constantly seen in my office. Lord Kelvin developed the second law using insights from Scripture that he summarized by quoting Psalm 102:26: "All of them shall wax old like a garment" (KJV).[7] In the past, the universe was more organized, so God must have "wound it up" like a clock at the beginning.

Physicists speculate about travel backward in time in the vicinity of black holes and wormholes. Such time travel presents several problems, however. It would complicate the concept of free will and result in an effect before a cause. Killing your mother before you were born would suddenly extinguish your own life and result in a paradox in logic.

Relative Time. Although the idea of time travel into the past raises many kinds of problems, the theory of special relativity predicts that time flows differently for two observers in motion with respect to each other. Salvador Dali artistically portrayed this warping of time in his painting *The Persistence of Memory.*★ C. S. Lewis uses this idea in creating the land of Narnia, where time moves at a different speed than in England.

According to special relativity, variations in time are noticeable at speeds close to that of light, so it isn't observable for ordinary human motion. Physicists, however, routinely detect it in devices known as particle accelerators. In my nuclear physics research pion particles that decayed in less than a microsecond when stationary in the laboratory appeared to take twice as long to decay when moving near the speed of light. According to experimentally confirmed general relativity, clock time moves slower in stronger gravitational fields as well.

Space and Time. General relativity theory also postulates extra space dimensions, though probably too small to be observed. The concept of extra space dimensions has been around since at least 1884, when the cleric Edwin A. Abbott published the classic *Flatland,* which describes zero-, one-, two-, three-, and four-dimensional worlds in a story format. These extra space dimensions may be useful in understanding how God works. He can be very close, for He is in "active communication with every part of His dominion"[8] without being perceived. Christ could walk through walls after His resurrection. The angel in Daniel 9 could fly all the way from heaven in three minutes, whereas it takes light eight minutes to get here just from the sun.

God's Relation to Human Time. Time is different for God than for humans (Ps. 90:4; 2 Peter 3:8).* One attempt to relate the two uses the Greek words *chronos* for human time and *kairos* for God's time.[9] In *chronos* time God works in natural, common, usual, and ordinary ways. But in *kairos* time He operates in a supernatural, uncommon, unusual, and extraordinary manner.[10] On a graph, cause-and-effect events *(chronos)* would lie on a continuous horizontal line, measurable by a clock or calendar, and be predictable and repeatable by science. On the same graph, unique, creative events *(kairos)* would plot as discontinuities in the line and be unpredictable and nonrepeatable. God doesn't usually bypass familiar natural law. To do so would remove our ability to do cause-and-effect reasoning. However, when He does act in nonrepeatable events instead of normal cause and effect, scientific reasoning will probably not be sufficient.

Other attempts have been made to explain the relation between God's time and human time. One analogy contrasts time for the author of a novel with time for characters in the novel. Authors have the whole plot in their heads at once, whereas the characters and readers have to go through the sequence of events in the book. An author could write two sentences several weeks apart that occur in an immediate sequence for the characters and the readers. Another explanation uses such illustrations as Supernovae 1987A. Astronomers observed this stellar explosion releasing billions of times the energy of the sun at an observatory in Chile on February 23, 1987. However, the explosion occurred 170,000 years before, with the light reaching our earth only recently. For God, who is present everywhere, both the explosion and the sighting on earth would be in the eternal now. But we humans perceive things within the aspects of past, present, and future.[11]

When the Creator intervenes in the creation, it may affect the rates at which things appear to happen. Humans, animals, and plants no doubt looked mature, or had an appearance of age, at the end of Creation week. Miracles such as the transformation of water into wine had a local effect on time, such that a biologist who examined the wine would have assumed that several months of biochemical activity would have taken place.

Augustine's answer to a question about time is an appropriate way to conclude: "If no one asks me, I know; if I wish to explain it to one that asketh, I know not."[12]

Arguments for God

We have been talking about God creating the universe. But how do we know that He even exists? People have attempted to demonstrate His existence in many ways. Some have argued that since the universe has a beginning (the cosmological argument) and that nature shows evidence of design (the teleological argument) He must be the one behind both facts. We will briefly mention two other arguments that people have employed to "prove" His existence.

The first has been called the ontological argument.* Anselm of Canterbury (1033-1109) first clearly described it. It begins by defining God as a being so great that nothing greater can be imagined. Next it recognizes that even an atheist admits that the idea of a God can exist in the mind. However, a deity who exists in reality is greater than one that exists only in the mind. Therefore, by definition God must exist in reality, not just in the mind. Alvin Plantinga finds this argument useful, but mainly for one who already believes.[13]

A second argument for God is based on goodness. Chapter 4 will discuss the reasoning many employ against the reality of God based on the ubiquitous presence of evil. But it is a two-edged sword. We could also argue for God by pointing to the undeniable goodness we see around us. Is it really necessary to survival that my taste buds enjoy lush blueberries or German chocolate cake so much? Is there a logical reason animals and humans play for the sheer enjoyment of it? What material benefit do I gain from seeing Michelangelo's *David* or hearing Handel's *Messiah?* Much of the creation is not strictly necessary. As Yancey says: "Evil's greatest triumph may be its success in portraying religion as an enemy of pleasure when, in fact, religion accounts for its source: every good thing that we enjoy is the invention of a Creator who lavished gifts on the world."[14]

All these arguments for God are not proofs, only clues. Immanuel Kant destroyed several of these arguments on rational grounds, although he himself believed in the existence of God for other reasons.[15] Such arguments are not part of science, for science is about finding naturalistic answers. They may require us to take a leap of faith, but it is at least reasonable. Pascal's wager suggests that it is smarter to bet on the existence of God: If we live our life as if there is a God and there *isn't,* we have just lost a few years and maybe not even that. If, however, we live our life as if there *isn't* a God and there is, we have lost eternity.*

When I wrote my doctoral dissertation, computer word processing was just becoming available. My fellow graduate students and I would jokingly wish for software that would print a final dissertation just by inserting the data and typing, "Do Thesis." Unfortunately, no such program was available, typing was boring, and one day I took a break to write the acknowledgments. I thanked the usual people, including my wife for her patience and a preschool daughter for keeping me excited about learning. Then I got the idea of including a paragraph of appreciation to God.

Nobody said anything about it until several years later. While attending some physics meetings, I went to an evening banquet and sat with a postdoctoral scientist who was doing research at the university I had attended as a graduate student. His wife mentioned that my name seemed familiar. Occasionally she would visit the physics laboratory and wait for her husband in the library. Having nothing else to do, she would look through the dissertation acknowledgments—the only nonphysics reading in the library. She had appreciated my mention of God:

"And finally, I would like to express my gratitude to the Creator for making our natural world such a fascinating topic for study; and for making the study of the great principles that govern the physical world an introduction and parallel to the great principles that guide our social activities and moral obligations, and a sampling of some small part of His character."

My acknowledgment was not a scientific statement, only a personal expression of faith. The design and the marvel of the universe and life *do not require* the Creator of Scripture, but they *are consistent with* the God depicted there.

A Theological Perspective of God as Creator in Genesis

Ancient cosmologies taught that the very fabric or structure of the universe had inherent in itself the capability to produce gods, matter, life, and everything else. In some ways the ancient concepts remind us of modern evolutionary theories that suggest that life came into being because of the inevitable outworking of natural physical laws. In fact, one Egyptologist has traced the concept of evolution all the way back to ancient Egypt.

Thus the Egyptians regarded the origin of the earth and its life as the result of natural forces, or laws, lurking within the cosmos itself. Once the first god emerged from the primeval chaos (often described as the watery turmoil the Egyptians observed during the annual flooding of the Nile), he created the other deities and everything else through one or more of a variety of processes. (Different gods would create in different ways.) One god named Ptah and worshiped particularly in the ancient Egyptian city of Memphis spoke everything into existence. He spoke, and the waters above separated from the waters below. Additional commands made dry land emerge and created living things, including human beings. At first glance the story of Ptah might remind us of the biblical account. But Ptah was quite different from the God of Genesis. First, he was not eternal, and came into being himself through the operation of natural blind forces. The cosmos just happened to have in itself the ability to originate gods. Second, Ptah did not create anything through any power in himself. When he "spoke," he was merely activating something that was already latent in the fabric of the universe. For example, if he said the word "tree," it had programmed in it—like some kind of cosmic DNA or digital code—the capacity to produce a tree when uttered. Third, neither Ptah nor anything he brought into existence was eternal. Everything, including the gods themselves, would eventually collapse back into the original chaos it had come from. Only the God of the Bible is everlasting (Ps. 90:1, 2; 93:2).

The Bible, however, portrays God as standing outside of and above all creation. He is not just some natural force at work, a product of creation itself. Also, the Lord creates through power that He personally possesses. He does not have to trigger some latent cosmic law that, once set in motion, automatically makes something spring into existence.

---

* See p. 17.

---

[1] Peter D. Ward and Donald Brownlee, *Rare Earth: Why Complex Life Is Uncommon in the Universe* (New York: Copernicus, 2000).

[2] In Henry Margenau and Roy Abraham Varghese, eds., *Cosmos, Bios, Theos: Scientists Reflect on Science, God, and the Origins of the Universe, Life, and Homo Sapiens* (La Salle, Ill.: Open Court, 1992), p. 78.

[3] Sir Fred Hoyle, *The Intelligent Universe* (New York: Holt, Rinehart and Winston, 1983), p. 19.

[4] Claire Ainsworth et al, "Life's Greatest Inventions," *New Scientist* 9 (April 2005): 26-35.

[5] Nancy R. Pearcey and Charles B. Thaxton, *The Soul of Science: Christian Faith and Natural Philosophy* (Wheaton, Ill.: Crossway Books, 1994), p. 254.

[6] David M. Raup, "Evolution and the Fossil Record," *Science* 213, no. 4505 (July 17,

1981): 289.

[7] Crosbie Smith and M. Norton Wise, *Energy and Empire: A Biographical Study of Lord Kelvin* (New York: Cambridge University Press, 1989), p. 317.

[8] E. G. White, *The Desire of Ages,* p. 356.

[9] Jack W. Provonsha, *A Remnant in Crisis* (Hagerstown, Md.: Review and Herald Pub. Assn., 1993), pp. 123-127; see also Madeleine L'Engle, *Walking on Water* (Colorado Springs, Colo.: WaterBrook Press, 1980), p. 103.

[10] See Ellen G. White, *Testimonies for the Church* (Mountain View, Calif.: Pacific Press Pub. Assn., 1948), vol. 8, pp. 259, 260.

[11] Philip Yancey, *Disappointment With God: Three Questions No One Asks Aloud* (Grand Rapids: Zondervan, 1988), pp. 230-232.

[12] *The Confessions* 11:14.

[13] Alvin Plantinga, *God, Freedom, and Evil* (Grand Rapids: Eerdmans, 1974), p. 112.

[14] Philip Yancey, *Soul Survivor: How My Faith Survived the Church* (New York: Doubleday, 2001), p. 55.

[15] Gunther S. Stent, *Paradoxes of Free Will* (Philadelphia: American Philosophical Society, 2002), p. 166.

3

The Creation of Humanity
Genesis 2

Mary Shelley describes how the scientist Victor Frankenstein infused "a spark of being into the lifeless thing that lay at [his] feet,"[1] creating a monster, a being so hideous that even he turned from it in disgust. The monster says to his maker, "I ought to be thy Adam,"[2] and pleads with Frankenstein for a companion, for "no Eve soothed my sorrows, nor shared my thoughts; I was alone. I remembered Adam's supplication to his Creator."[3] Finally the monster takes out his vengeance on his creator by murdering those family and friends that Frankenstein holds most dear.

Not long before writing her book, Mary Shelley read *Paradise Lost* and used Milton's themes of human creation and evil in her depiction of Frankenstein's creation of the monster.

The previous chapter centered on God, the transcendental Creator. The second chapter of Genesis focuses on human beings and our relationships to other humans, the world, good and evil, and God. Unlike Frankenstein, God created humanity perfect (Gen. 2:7, 21, 22) and provided human companionship (verses 18, 23-25), a good world (verses 8-14), work and purpose (verses 5, 15, 19, 20), and moral guidance (verses 16, 17).

Human Characteristics

God created humanity in His own image, uniquely different from animals, for "one eats animals but sleeps with persons; any inversion of this procedure is apt to occasion considerable attention."[4] Exact definitions of personhood become important not only in understanding Scripture but also when discussing such issues as cloning, abortion, and euthanasia.★ Jesus revealed the perfect human and came to restore that image in us.[5] The first humans received a good body and a conscious mind with a reason for living and the free will to carry it out. God created them for relationships and with their own ability to create.★

Body and Mind. The Western world has considered two main explanations for the relationship between body and mind. The first is that of dualism. Propounded by the Greek philosopher Plato, it separates body from mind/soul. René Descartes famously differentiated mind from matter: "I think, therefore I am." The second concept, known as monism, holds that only the physical is real. Thinking is no more than physicochemical interactions, and we can explain human behavior mechanistically. The difference between humans and animals is one not of kind, but only of evolutionary degree.

Genesis 2 outlines a wholistic explanation for the relation between body and mind—God breathed into the body, and the first man became a living soul. Thus human nature includes concepts from dualism (both body and consciousness) and monism (a single living being), but goes beyond both. To use an analogy, physical hardware plus "mental" software make up a "living," working computer.

A Good Body. God's original creation of the human body was very good. Christ showed His respect for it by forever taking on human, material existence (John 1:14).[6] The fact that our bodies are God's temples gives us reason for healthful living and for continuing the healing ministry of Christ. It is the human body that He will resurrect to immortality.

A disrespect for the material body produced several ancient heresies. Manicheaism's goal was to free the spirit from the body. Gnostics feared matter as inherently evil, leading them to the extremes of either asceticism or licentiousness. They felt they had privileged information about the creation of the natural world, historical events, and the future. Docetists believed that Jesus only seemed to have a real body, and thus they saw no importance in learning about the material world, creativity, society, or history.[7]

A Conscious Mind. Weinberg says that for the materialist "it is consciousness that presents us with the greatest difficulty."[8] We cannot explain consciousness naturalistically. It is a domain closed to science.

The mind, although not located in physical space, does exist in physical time. The past is retained only in memory. The present is embedded in a continuous flow of events, such that pain endurable for a moment can become unendurable over time. Future purpose gives meaning to the present and in at least one sense inverts the usual relationship of cause and effect because *future* goals determine *present* actions.

The mind recognizes truth, but as Pilate asked, "What is truth?" (John 18:38). It is more than merely statements provable by logic. In fact, Gödel's incompleteness theorem (1931) states that in any system rich enough to be interesting true statements will exist that are not provable.⋆

The mind perceives concepts as a whole, not just as the sum of pieces. The intellect recognizes the full optical illusion of M. C. Escher's *Waterfall*⋆ as impossible even though individual parts look reasonable. The mind also identifies statements that are neither true nor false when looked at as a whole. For example, Paul wrote that "one of their own prophets [Epimenides] has said, 'Cretans are always liars'" (Titus 1:12, NIV). If Epimenides is always a liar, his statement itself is a lie. But if the statement is false, then Cretans are not always liars. I think you begin to see the problem here.

We cannot explain consciousness through the approach known as reductionism, that is, trying to deal with it as nothing more than the results of biochemical reactions in the brain's neurons. The whole mind is more than the sum of its parts. Language, foresight, art appreciation, emotions, and self-awareness cannot be reduced to just cellular interactions or computer artificial intelligence. One finds similar emergent properties in a novel with the story being more than just spelling and grammar. Thus consciousness is more than life, and life itself more than matter.

Purpose. Humanity's purpose is "higher than the highest human thought."[9] "The mysteries of the visible universe . . . invited man's study. . . . Heart-to-heart communion with his Maker was his high privilege."[10] Unfortunately, the perspective of naturalism—restricting reality to nothing more than matter and energy—changed this worldview. The Copernican revolution removed the earth from being the center of the universe, and later developments explained how it might form by natural processes. Next, science recognized that the physical and chemical laws and biological processes of nature also applied to humans. Finally life was assumed to form by process. Although helpful in understanding many things, this progression taken to its extreme of a purely mechanistic universe governed by chance leaves humanity meaningless.

A desolate piece penned by Bertrand Russell entitled "A Free Man's Worship"⋆ reaches the conclusion that "only on the firm foundation of unyielding despair can the soul's habitation henceforth be safely built." Fortunately, other philosophical options give us both purpose and freedom.

Free Will. While the cause-and-effect relations of the physical world do influence the body, human free will means that the mind's decisions are not totally restricted by matter and energy. A certain freedom from outside circumstances is necessary in human decision-making if the individual is to really have any moral responsibility for the actions he or she takes.

Because human free will makes possible a physical effect without a physical cause, the physical universe is not totally deterministic.* Thus humans are unique. They can freely select how they will respond to God's purpose for their creation.

Relationships to Other Humans

The Creator is a God of love, a plural, for love requires more than one person. *Love* is a transitive verb needing both a subject and an object. "God said, 'Let *us* make humankind in *our* image'" (Gen. 1:26). God wanted creatures on whom to bestow His love. Humans, made in His image, also have the capacity for loving relationships in marriage, the family, the church, and even to those who are different.

Male and female together represent the image of God, for "in the image of God he created him; male and female" (verse 27) and He "called them 'man'" (Gen. 5:2, NIV). Adam saw that the animals had mates and realized that he too needed companionship. I remember seeing everyone else getting married in college and realizing that I too longed for a companion. My bride and I put on our wedding announcements: "It is not good that man should be alone." *That Friday in Eden* describes that companionship.[11] The book begins with one of the "things" that amazed the wise man—"the way of a man with a girl" (Prov. 30:19)—and goes on to use the Song of Solomon to show the beauty of the marriage relationship. Covenant agreement appears throughout Genesis, and it first occurs here with the "cleaving" together of the marriage covenant.

Genesis describes the beginnings of still other relationships. A couple was to leave parents to set up a home and be fruitful and multiply. Once sin intruded, however, it shattered relationships, and their restoration is the theme of the rest of the Bible. It is good for people to dwell together in unity (Ps. 133), and the early church grew when they were in "one accord" (Acts 1:14, KJV; 2:1; 4:32). John Donne's meditation recognizes that "no man is an island."*

Both the scientific community and the church feel a worldwide family spirit. I participated in a nuclear physics experiment at a U.S. national laboratory where both an Arab and an Israeli were congenially involved. I discovered the intricacies of the Adventist world family when I purchased a book for my daughter while lecturing at Helderberg College in South Africa. A visiting Newbold College professor from England offered to deliver the book to her son, who would then pass it on to my daughter, both of whom were living in Oxford.

Naturalistic Basis for Relationships. The ethical implications for Christians from a recent field of study known as sociobiology may be greater than from any other area of science. Sociobiology treats human and animal behavior as resulting solely from interactions between genes and the environment,[12] with morality evolving as an instinct.[13]

The seminal book by Edward Wilson entitled *Sociobiology*[14] describes such social animal interactions as communication, aggression, social spacing, roles and castes, and paternal care in organisms such as bee colonies and ape families. Comparing and contrasting these behaviors between animals and humans, he claims, gives us insight into social evolution and sociology.

Wilson explains how altruistic (unselfish) behaviors might have developed using totally naturalistic, evolutionary assumptions. Normally the evolutionary maxim survival of the fittest suggests selfish competition between individuals, with only the fittest individuals living long enough to pass on their genes. Sociobiology suggests that survival of the fittest can also refer to the fittest group surviving by being selfish as a group but altruistic to individuals in the group. While endangering their own lives, a mother bird protects its young, and a single prairie dog whistles to warn the colony, because the survival of the genes of several offspring or other relatives is more evolutionarily advantageous than the survival of a single individual. This theory for the evolution of altruistic behavior dawned on the scientist J.B.S. Haldane while drinking at a pub. He calculated that others could pass on his genes, so he blurted out, "I am willing to die for four uncles or eight cousins."[15]

These ideas have come to form the basis for a number of ethics books,[16] although even Wilson recognizes that this purposeless worldview could result in "the rapid dissolution of transcendental goals toward which societies can organize."[17]

Christian Basis for Relationships. In the original creation nothing lived for itself. Animal, plant, and ocean—all took to give.[18] The Christian basis of human relationships is this law of love in the heart (Matt. 22:37-39; Rom. 13:8, 10; John 13:35; 1 John 4:7), not an external law (2 Cor. 3:6) or religious ritual (Micah 6:6-8) or knowledge (1 Cor. 8:1; 13:1-3). For three years in academy our team of two won the unionwide Bible contest. But by the end of the third year, it had become clear to me that knowing the facts wasn't nearly as important as having the right relationships.

During high school my classmates and I discussed whether a universe could be constructed on indifference or hate instead of love. As I later studied physics I found that the forces governing human relationships are analogous to those regulating natural relationships. Gravity holds the sun and earth together and keeps people attached to earth. The electromagnetic force binds electrons and protons together in the atom, making chemistry possible. The strong force keeps the protons in the nucleus together. One particle, the neutrino, interacts weakly. It doesn't hurt anything—millions of them pass through us every second—but it isn't of much use, either. Repulsive forces keep everything from collapsing, but the attractive forces determine most important interactions. For the universe to work, laws governing relationships are necessary for both particles and people.

The fundamental beliefs of the church involve people relationships. The Sabbath is concerned with how people are treated (Isa. 58), and Jesus used the day for many acts of healing (Matt. 12:10-13; Luke 4:31-39; 13:10-13; 14:1-6; John 5:1-16; 7:23). The everlasting gospel for the whole world (Rev. 14:6) includes the story of the gift of love by the woman who washed Jesus' feet (Matt. 26:13). God's final communication to the world will include the Elijah message, the restoration of relationships (Mal. 4:5, 6). When the hour of judgment takes place, it will be based on how we treated the least among us (Matt. 25:31-46).

Relating to Those Who Are Different. Although people in Jesus' day feared to mingle with the Gentiles or even many of their own nation, Christ developed relationships with publicans, prostitutes, lepers, Samaritans, Greeks, and the Syrophoenician woman. He made His most scathing rebukes against those indifferent to these relationships: the accusers of the woman taken in adultery (John 8); the religious leaders evicted when He cleansed the Temple; and the Pharisees who took widows' fortunes, misrepresented God to proselytes, and omitted judgment and mercy (Matt. 23).

When I was preparing to do graduate work at a secular university, a respected Adventist professor encouraged me to become part of that university's community. The advice paid off. Plenty of positive opportunities presented themselves for interaction as my university colleagues and I would spend weeks together at various research labs working on experiments, eating, sharing motel rooms, and relaxing.

Relating on Origins Issues. The Bible and church history provide examples of how to deal with potentially divisive issues. The Jerusalem Council decided how the church would incorporate Gentile Christians (Acts 15). Melanchthon tried to mediate between Luther, who held to a more literal interpretation of the Eucharist ("This is my body" [Matt. 26:26, KJV]), and Zwingli, who viewed it more metaphorically.[19]

We can learn much from these situations on how to discuss the issues, questions, and problems of our understanding of how God created our world. A balanced approach to any important belief combines both certainty and flexibility, both the authority of the corporate body and the uniqueness of individual beliefs, and both the firm foundation and landmarks on the one hand[20] and growth, progress, and new light on the other.[21] Such a perspective makes it harder to say, "I'm right; you're different; therefore you must be wrong," and easier to say, "God's right, but we're both incomplete." I pray that as we study the Creator's handiwork, we will build bridges to each other instead of walls between us.

Relationship to the World

When God looked at everything He had made, "behold, it was very good" (Gen. 1:31, KJV). It was a creation not to be worshipped, but to be honored. God then gave humanity dominion over this creation—their work of caring for the earth. Study of this good world is worthwhile and required for good stewardship among God's people.

Naming. The lengthy descriptions in Genesis about naming things may puzzle the modern reader. But the ancient world considered it an important activity. Naming in biblical times demonstrated authority and relationship. God's words created the world, and He did the first naming in Genesis 1 (of day and night and of the heavens, earth, and seas). Adam fittingly named the animals, for he understood their nature. He called his companion "woman" and eventually named her Eve. "To name is to love,"[22] as happily married couples who have endearing names for each other know, whereas slaves in Roman times often received only numbers (e.g., Quartus [Rom. 16:23]). When God entered into a covenant with Abram and Jacob, He changed their names. The moment of truth for the blind and deaf Helen Keller came when she could name the water she felt rushing against her hand at the water pump. She now had a new sense of control over her world.

Dominion. Thus the most important aspect of naming from the perspective of the biblical mind was that it gave authority over something. The earth and its life belong to God (Gen. 14:19, 22; Ex. 9:29; Deut.

10:14; Ps. 24:1; 50:10, 11; 95:5; 1 Cor. 10:26). He cares for His creation (Matt. 6:26; Ps. 147:9), but gave us dominion over it (Gen. 1:28; 2:15).

The atmosphere, water, land, and climate, as well as the diversity of life and energy resources, are part of our dominion.[23] Agriculture and deforestation, manufacturing and industry, and human population growth have adversely affected our environment.

The threat of nuclear war concerns many, and the disposal of radioactive waste is a continuing problem for more developed nations. Visiting the Ukraine in the 1990s, I met a mother whose son had inhaled a great deal of radioactive material and suffered from respiratory ailments after the Chernobyl disaster. More recently I arranged for a theology and science group to visit the Waste Isolation Pilot Plant (WIPP) near Carlsbad, New Mexico, which stores 55-gallon drums of low-level nuclear waste in a salt layer a half-mile underground.★

Care for the environment has close ties to several doctrines[24] besides creation: 1. The Sabbath gives us and the whole of creation[25] rest from our greed. 2. The nonimmortality of the soul contrasts with the belief of dualism, which treats the physical as less important. 3. In the eschatology scenario of Revelation, God will "destroy them which destroy the earth" (Rev. 11:18, KJV). 4. The health message reminds us that the sacred body temple requires pure air, water, and food. 5. Special concern for the poor means care for the environment, since pollution hurts the poor the most.

What are Adventists doing to care for the environment? The General Conference has an official statement on stewardship of creation.★ Walla Walla College offers an environmental science major.★ And individual church members can avoid waste and its resulting damage on the world around us by simple living, following the principle of reduce, reuse, and recycle.

Relationship to Good and Evil

Free Choice. The tree of knowledge provided the first human pair with an alternative choice. As part of His image, God endowed humanity with free will, but not all of His knowledge. Nor did He implant in them an unchangeable character. Instead, He gave them the freedom to develop their own characters.

Humans want freedom, but it can in some ways be a burden, because it entails responsibility. Behind every dictatorship lurks the belief that people really don't want freedom and its inherent responsibility.[26] In Fyodor Dostoyevsky's *The Brothers Karamazov* a cardinal during the Spanish Inquisition "claims it as a merit for himself and his church that at last they have vanquished freedom and have done so to make men happy." However, if people do not bear responsibility for their choices, wrong as well as right, "any shred of free will left in the human being is taken away."[27]

Science fiction, as well as real life, provide horrendous examples of restrictive dictators and government systems that seek to control the minds of fellow humans. George Orwell's *1984* portrays a totalitarian society ruled by an organization called Big Brother, which censors all behavior and thought. The main character becomes subversive, is caught and charged with thought crimes, and is then sent for rehabilitation to the Ministry of Love, where its agents torture him until his thoughts coincide with the party line. Fortunately, God's government doesn't work that way.

God made Adam aware of the results of his free choice beforehand, results from natural consequence, not divine favoritism or vengeance. Human beings must realize what their choices will lead to, or they are not truly free. This requires a dependable, law-based universe in which actions have real consequences. Thus dealing with the results of free choice must be part of any human system of justice.

Relationship to God

Our relationship to God manifests itself in how we respond to His divine law, His physical creation, and His image in other humans. To provide special opportunities for relating to them, He set aside sacred space (first in the Garden of Eden and later at the tabernacle and Temple) and sacred time during yearly festivals and on the Sabbath.

The Garden of Eden presented rich sanctuary symbolism with its cherubim and light, eastern entrance, rivers and water, gold and precious stones, a tree (echoing the lampstand), a place for evening communion with God, and after sin an altar at the entrance.[28]

Creation week culminated with the Sabbath, also rich in symbolic meaning. The fourth commandment differs from the others in being a memorial. It began at Creation and is literally applicable only to this earth.

The basis for the weekly cycle is independent of the astronomical motions that govern the cycles of day, month, and year. The seven-day cycle of Scripture has become universally accepted, although the name for each day in the Western world comes from the European names for the seven wandering celestial bodies: Sun, Moon, Mars, Mercury, Jupiter, Venus, and Saturn.[29] Ancient cultures had other than seven-day cycles. Market weeks three to five days long developed in the Americas, Southeast Asia, and Africa. The weekly cycle consisted of eight days in Italy, 12 in China, and 19 for the Baha'i.[30] After the general emergence of the seven-day cycle some groups attempted to change it. During the French Revolution in the late eighteenth century the government set up the metric system. The meter and gram stuck, but not the Republican calendar* with its 10-day week.[31] In the early part of the twentieth century the Soviet Union established a five-day workweek, but that too disappeared.

Sabbath Symbolism. As for any symbol, the Sabbath can become useless when separated from what it represents. However, celebration of the Sabbath can be very meaningful when we keep in mind the reality that the Sabbath symbolizes:

1. We need rest because of our limited abilities, especially from a spiritual viewpoint. The Sabbath reminds us that we can rest from trying to gain God's approval. Christ is Creator, and only He can re-create us from our fallen condition to a righteous one (Ex. 31:13). We rest because God has given us freedom from slavery both in the past (Deut. 5:15) and in the future. And we can rest from trying to explain everything in the natural world, including the details of how God created and flooded this earth.

2. Humanity is to worship the Creator (Ex. 20:11; Rev. 14:6, 7), not the creation (especially the creature or beast of Revelation 14:9). But that is sometimes easier said than done. Those who accept Scripture solely on the basis of the scientific evidence, for example, can, I believe, unwittingly worship creation instead of God Himself.

3. God is wiser than humanity (1 Cor. 1:17-31, especially verse 25). For many of His requirements, we can obey out of understanding. But at times we obey even when we do not completely comprehend why. Thus we can worship on the seventh day even if we do not understand exactly how or what God created during those seven days of creation.

4. God is Lord of time, as He is Lord of all else. Because He owns all, so we are to be good stewards of all. God owns our bodies as the temple of the Holy Spirit (1 Cor. 6:19, 20), so we keep them healthy. The Lord owns our talents that produce income, so we use that money wisely (Deut. 8, especially verse 18). He also owns all time (Ps. 90:4; 1 Tim. 1:17; 2 Peter 3:8), so we use it wisely, but especially the seventh day of the week (Gen. 2:2, 3), so we keep it holy.

5. The Creator is a personal God who has set aside a time to be with us, just as He set aside a space in the tabernacle (Ex. 25:8). That time is a delight (Isa. 58:13, 14) and for our benefit (Mark 2:27). It is a sign of His covenant with us (Ex. 31:13, 16) and of our belonging to Him (Eze. 20:20). As a friend we spend time with Him out of love, not from a forced

allegiance or fear of punishment. Jesus wanted to be with us, so He hid His glory in human flesh (John 1:14). He is Immanuel, God with us (Matt. 1:23). And finally in the New Jerusalem God will live with us forever (Rev. 21:3).

The Sabbath is a symbol of everything discussed in Genesis 2. It reminds us of our human limitations, our recognition of God's Creatorship, our acknowledgment of His greatness, our role as stewards, and of the importance of personal relationships both on the human and divine-human levels.

A Theological Perspective of the Sabbath and God's People

God created the first human beings and then rested on the Sabbath, establishing a pattern that continues throughout the rest of the Bible. Not only did the Lord create people in the first place, but the Sabbath also symbolizes His power to restore them. People and Sabbath thus become the two sides of a single coin.

When human beings rebelled, God did not abandon them. He still sought a people for Himself. After the Flood He called Abram to begin that people anew. Eventually His people went into Egypt, where slavery almost destroyed them. They forgot who they were. The Lord had to instill in them a sense of identity as His people. As He led them through the wilderness He assured them that He would care for them through the regular gift of manna (Ex. 16:13-36). Their obedience to the manna cycle and their rest on the Sabbath became a test of their acceptance of God as their Lord and they themselves as His people.

At Sinai God declared them "a holy nation" (Ex. 19:6, NIV). They now existed only because He had delivered them from the bondage and the chaos of slavery (Ex. 20:2; Deut. 5:15)—He had created them as a people anew. There He proclaimed the Ten Commandments, including the Sabbath one. Once again observance of the Sabbath symbolized their acknowledgment of their peoplehood.

Not only was the Sabbath prominent in the formation of God's people; it also surfaces in Scripture whenever they face the threat of destruction, assimilation, or dispersion. For example, 2 Kings 11 tells how Athaliah, the queen mother of Judah's King Ahaziah and daughter of Ahab and Jezebel of Israel, seized control of Judah after her son's death. She tried to destroy all members of the royal family. But Ahaziah's sister, Jehosheba, managed to save Ahaziah's son, Joash, and hid him in the Temple precincts for six years. In the seventh year (an interesting echo of Creation week) Jehoiada, the high priest, staged a coup to remove the queen from power and place Joash on the throne. The coup took place on the Sabbath (2 Kings 11:5-9). After the execution of Athaliah, Jehoiada made "a covenant, between the Lord and the king and people, that they should be the Lord's people" (verse 17, KJV).

By mentioning the Sabbath along with the establishment of a covenant, the biblical author directs our attention back to the Sinai experience. The people whom Athaliah had almost destroyed through her pagan activities God now reconstitutes and brings back into renewed relationship with Him.

The book of Isaiah shows how resident aliens and eunuchs, both regarded as outsiders

---

or at least second-class citizens, can through Sabbath observance become part of God's people (Isa. 56). Sabbath observance also forms part of the prophet's discussion of true worship (Isa. 58), and true worship consists of a proper relationship with God and with fellow humanity. Isaiah also declares that God's people will go into exile because of their national rebellion, but when He restores them with the rest of humanity in a new earth, they will from Sabbath to Sabbath worship the Lord (Isa. 66:23). Then, just before the destruction of Jerusalem by Babylon, the prophet Jeremiah also emphasizes the Sabbath (Jer. 17:19-27). Judah faced extinction as a nation and even as a people. If they would honor the Sabbath, however, Jerusalem would be inhabited forever (verses 24-26). But they refused to listen to the prophet and went into captivity.

In Ezekiel God sketches the history of His people before announcing that He will restore Israel, bringing them back from exile (Eze. 20). Twice He mentions that the Sabbath was a sign or symbol of His relationship to them as a people (verses 12, 20). When some did return from Babylon, the Sabbath again made its appearance in Scripture. As Nehemiah worked to rebuild the identity of religious life in Jerusalem (religion was one of the most important aspects of all ancient self-identity) he found that its inhabitants, in league with the pagan people around them, had turned the Sabbath into just another market day (Neh. 13:15-22).

The context of the incident is the danger of assimilation that threatens the people of Jerusalem. Non-Israelites were moving into the city and even the Temple precincts (verses 1-9). Many of God's people, including one of the sons of the high priest, had non-Israelite wives (verses 23-30). The children could not even speak their fathers' language (language is also a vital part of any group's self-awareness). God's people were vanishing as an identifiable body. To stop the destructive process Nehemiah stressed the Sabbath as a symbol of their identity as God's people and of their allegiance to Him.

---

* See p. 17.

---

[1] Mary Shelley, *Frankenstein; or, the Modern Prometheus* (1818), p. 51.

[2] *Ibid.*, p. 89.

[3] *Ibid.*, p. 117.

[4] I. G. Stent, *Paradoxes of Free Will*, p. 79.

[5] E. G. White, *The Desire of Ages*, p. 37; *Education*, p. 16.

[6] White, *The Desire of Ages*, p. 25.

[7] Mark A. Noll, *The Scandal of the Evangelical Mind* (Grand Rapids: Eerdmans, 1994), pp. 47-54.

[8] S. Weinberg, *Dreams of a Final Theory*, p. 44.

[9] White, *Education*, p. 18.

[10] *Ibid.*, p. 15.

[11] Alberta Mazat, *That Friday in Eden* (Mountain View, Calif.: Pacific Press Pub. Assn., 1981).

[12] Ronald L. Carter, "Do Genes Determine Morality?" *College and University Dialogue* 5, no. 3 (1993): 5-8.

[13] Edward O. Wilson, *On Human Nature* (Cambridge, Mass.: Harvard University Press, 1978), pp. 5, 208.

[14] Wilson, *Sociobiology: The New Synthesis* (Cambridge, Mass.: Harvard University Press, 1975).

[15] In Mary Midgley, *Evolution as a Religion: Strange Hopes and Stranger Fears* (New York: Methuen, 1985), p. 121.

[16] Leonard R. Brand and Ronald L. Carter, "Sociobiology: The Evolution Theory's Answer to Altruistic Behavior," *Origins* 19, no. 2 (1992): 64, 65.

[17] Wilson, *On Human Nature*, p. 4.

[18] White, *The Desire of Ages*, pp. 20, 21; see also Prov. 11:24.

[19] Williston Walker et al., *A History of the Christian Church*, 4th ed. (New York: Charles Seribner's Sons, 1985), pp. 445, 446, 456, 457, 527.

[20] White, *Counsels to Writers and Editors*, pp. 30, 31.

[21] *Ibid.*, pp. 32-42.

[22] Madeleine L'Engle, *Walking on Water*, p. 130.

[23] William C. Clark, "Managing Planet Earth," *Scientific American* 261, no. 3 (September 1989): 46-54.

[24] A. Josef Greig, "Our Poisoned Planet," *Adventist Review*, Apr. 19, 1990, pp. 15-18.

[25] God commanded a Sabbath rest for the land (Lev. 25:3-22; 2 Chron. 36:20, 21) and the animals (Ex. 20:10).

[26] L'Engle, pp. 115, 116.

[27] *Ibid.*, p. 217.

[28] Ellen G. White, *Patriarchs and Prophets* (Mountain View, Calif.: Pacific Press Pub. Assn., 1890), pp. 83, 84; Laurence Turner, *Back to the Present* (Grantham, Eng.: Autumn House, 2004), pp. 41-43; Gordon J. Wenham, *Word Biblical Commentary: Genesis 1-15* (Waco, Tex.: Word Books, 1987), pp. 61-65.

[29] Eviatar Zerubavel, *The Seven Day Circle: The History and Meaning of the Week* (New York: Free Press, 1985), p. 13.

[30] *Ibid.*, pp. 44ff.

[31] *Ibid.*, pp. 27ff.

4

Senseless Suffering

Genesis 3; 4

On several occasions I have worked with a theoretical nuclear physicist at Moscow State University. During one of our conversations Dr. Goncharova asked about the problem of suffering. I was ready to tell her of God's wanting free creatures to love Him and the results of poor choices. However, she had attended the local Adventist church, so before I could start she said, "I already know about the fallen angel." Immediately I knew my nicely packaged theoretical answer didn't meet her personal need.

She had lived through years of Communist oppression. Even while I was there she was struggling to take care of her husband, who had just suffered an unnecessary heart attack. The doctors knew of his risk, but only after the attack could they legally admit him to the hospital for treatment. What senseless suffering! Since that visit I have done a great deal of thinking and reading about the problem of evil . . . and experiencing some of its results. I spent more than three years with first my mom and then my dad fighting and finally succumbing to the ravages of cancer. Perhaps I could answer her question a little better now than I did then.

Genesis 2 paints a perfect world; Genesis 3 depicts its brokenness. Both chapters begin with an ideal garden and a tree of life, but the third chapter ends with God's driving the human pair out so they won't eat the fruit of that tree. God creates the human pair for relationships, only to have the couple shatter all those relationships. In Genesis 4 the brokenness extends to Cain and Lamech.

Temptation

People have struggled for centuries to understand how evil could enter and destroy a perfect world. Often they pattern their understanding after the account in Genesis 3. In his attempt to portray the temptation of a perfect couple, C. S. Lewis tells the story of the newly created king and queen who live on the floating islands of the planet Perelandra. Their creator has permitted them to visit the Fixed Land, but prohibited them from sleeping there. The two become separated after accidentally finding themselves on two separate islands. A human agent of evil from earth becomes the Unman and tempts the queen to enjoy the certainty of living on the Fixed Land. This temptation for certainty expands into a desire for ownership and for enough control to repeat pleasurable experiences. In conversation with the queen, the Unman's statements are always very nearly true.

Another human, a man from earth named Ransom, aids the woman in resisting the temptation and in so doing receives a wound in the heel. Ransom explains that in other matters, obedience involves what seems reasonable. Only with respect to the Fixed Land can the queen taste the real joy of obeying, because only here is her creator's bidding the only reason for obedience. Several times in answering the Unman's arguments Ransom feels that telling the truth will be fatal, but even so "only truth would serve." Lewis's tale ends more happily than Genesis 3.

The story of Frankenstein, on the other hand, does not have a happy ending. Victor Frankenstein seeks knowledge of nature's physical secrets and wants to "pioneer a new way, explore unknown powers, and unfold to the world the deepest mysteries of creation."[1] After succumbing to the lure of science, he advises others to "avoid ambition, even if it be only the apparently innocent one of distinguishing yourself in science and discoveries."[2]

All such tales are only echoes of the Genesis 3 account. Let us now look at the scriptural story itself.

The Serpent. The trickster theme is a common motif in world literature, including the biblical stories of deception by Abraham, Rachel, and Jacob. The Old Testament does not attempt to explain the trickster serpent in Genesis 3, but Jesus refers to the devil as the father of lies (John 8:44), and Revelation equates the ancient serpent with the devil and Satan (Rev. 12:9).

The Truth. The talking serpent who seduced Eve was a subtle liar. In Paradise Lost the serpent's eloquent speech astonished her, making her think that eating the fruit might do even more for her than for the serpent.[3] The tempter began by asking a deceptive question: "Did God say, 'You shall not eat from any tree in the garden?'" (Gen. 3:1). Eagerly the woman came to God's defense and zealously replied that they were not even to touch the forbidden fruit (verse 3), thus expanding God's prohibition.[4]

This first great deception was a half truth, not a total falsehood. Evil has no independent existence, but is always distorted good. As such, it warns us to tell "the truth, the whole truth, and nothing but the truth" as we study the issues of origins. Exaggerated claims for data and misrepresentation of opponents are constant temptations for many creationists. Ian Plimer graphically portrays this perception of creationists in his book *Telling Lies for God.*[5]

The Appeal. All the trees that God created were good for food and pleasant to the eye (Gen. 2:9), but Eve also found the forbidden fruit desirable to make one wise (Gen. 3:6). The fruit had a threefold appeal to practical needs, aesthetic needs, and the desire for control and power: the lust of the flesh, the lust of the eye, and the pride of life, as 1 John 2:16 puts it. Sin takes the normal physical needs and perverts them into a craving for instant gratification. It transforms the enjoyment of beauty into an insatiable desire for luxury. And it alters our responsibility as divinely appointed stewards into a lust for domination and abusive control.

Jesus, the Second Adam, faced the same three temptations in the wilderness: bread for food, an attention-capturing spectacle at the Temple, and illicitly acquired power over the world. Instead of taking the path of suffering, Jesus was tempted to be the expected Jewish Messiah, or, as Dostoyevsky summarizes it, one who would use miracle, mystery, and authority. Satan suggested to Jesus that (1) He could miraculously remove the fear of want and provide for the Jews' physical desires. But, as Dostoyevsky* phrases it, "thou wouldst not enslave man by a miracle, and didst crave faith given freely." That (2) He could affirm their spiritual life with a mysterious and spectacular announcement of His mission at the Temple; but He demonstrated restraint. That (3) He could authoritatively conquer their enemies and cure the world's problems in His lifetime; but He resisted the "savior complex" of providing all the answers with certainty, of irrefutably proving who He was, and of compelling belief by silencing all skeptics.[6]

Today we also would like to improve on Christ's methods by borrowing "the tools of manipulation perfected by politicians, salesmen, and advertising copywriters."[7] We would like a miracle to provide undeniable explanations of the origin of life and matter. Modern Christians find themselves tempted with the lure of having the inside track and the power such knowledge brings. The desire for an all-encompassing knowledge of "good and evil" tempts us all, but the one who considered himself "as wise as god" eventually lost Eden (see Eze. 28:6, 12-16).

Evil Results for Living Organisms

We will now examine some of the effects that sin has had on the world around us—living organisms in this chapter and the physical world in the next chapter. The candirú catfish, for example, will lodge itself in the urethra of a swimmer by extending its spines, producing an excruciating pain that only surgical removal of the creature will stop.* A tiny fly, the cecidomyian gall midge, at times will reproduce asexually at such an early stage of its life that its offspring will devour it from the inside.[8] Predation and parasitism offer countless other examples. In 1803 Charles Darwin's grandfather, Erasmus Darwin, observed that such things in nature make it "one great slaughterhouse."*

Charles Darwin himself found it difficult to believe that a benevolent God was the source of parasitism, the death of his child from typhoid, or the everlasting punishment that the "plain language" of the Bible describes. In an 1860 letter Darwin said, "I cannot persuade myself that a beneficent and omnipotent God would have designedly created the Ichneumonidae with the express intention of their feeding within the living bodies of caterpillars or that a cat should play with mice."* He felt that natural law, indifferent to the cruelty and pain of nature and to human misery, provided a better answer than blaming such things directly on God.

After wrestling with this terrible problem, Darwin developed a mechanism for the origin of species based on natural law. It stated that from the overproduction of offspring, only the fittest survive by natural selection in the struggle for existence. Tennyson gave poetic form to the concept in his poem *In Memoriam*★ when he spoke of "nature, red in tooth and claw."

Social Darwinism. These concepts eventually led to the theory of social Darwinism, which put progress through struggle into the political and socioeconomic sciences. Although the idea of struggle long predates Darwin, he provided an argument from nature to show that it is natural and good. While Darwin himself did not support social Darwinism, the full title of his famous book was on the *Origin of Species by Means of Natural Selection, or, the Preservation of Favored Races in the Struggle for Life.*★

Before Darwin, racist biologists had argued in support of slavery, colonialism, and war against American Indians, but social Darwinism gave them new ammunition for their theories. German biologist Ernst Haeckel developed Darwin's ideas into the concept of a superior race, and his writings were one of many factors leading to the two world wars of the twentieth century. The concept of competition was part of the title for Hitler's book *Mein Kampf,* which means "my struggle," and Mao Tse-tung regarded German Darwinism as the foundation of Chinese scientific socialism.

Eugenics, or artificial selection for humans, developed into a movement in northern Europe and the United States during the early twentieth century. It was based on the work of Darwin's cousin Francis Galton. Concluding that inheritance had a large role in disease, pauperism, imbecility, criminality, and immorality, some countries instituted forced sterilization of such people. After World War II, however, such ideas lost much of their popularity.

Karl Marx, whose writings form the basis for socialism and communism, saw in Darwin's theory of competition and evolution in nature a basis for his own theory of class struggle and historical development among humans. Much of the world's commerce today is based on capitalism, the economic form of struggle and survival of the fittest. As we see, Darwinian theory has had a powerful influence on world history.

Death. Death is an integral part of nature, but even so we have difficulty relating to its mystery. Some, like the Los Angeles County coroner's office★ with its online gift shop, treat it humorously. Others, such as Elisabeth Kubler-Ross, who has written on near-death experiences, understand it to be a transition into another existence.

But what is death and what does the Bible mean when it says "death came through sin" (Rom. 5:12)? Modern scientific definitions for death are not always equivalent to those of Bible writers. Clearly the book of Romans does not have in mind the death of plant tissue, since God provided the first pair with many fruits to eat, and digestion breaks down plant cells.

Cell death, or apoptosis, is programmed into organisms and is necessary for life.[9] In the developing fetus, certain cells die on the hand to separate the fingers. The lining of the digestive system dies and sloughs off regularly. The skin's outer layer of dead cells forms a protection for the rest of the body. Body cells often mutate, but a built-in surveillance system directs such cells to die. When that system doesn't work, cancer results. Death seems to be a necessary part of the ecosystem, and even pain has an important part to play in survival.

We may be comfortable with the death of cells and fruit before sin, but not of humans. In between these two extremes, an ascending level of unpleasantness, suffering, and death is related to fruit remnants and their decay, plant tissues such as flowers or leaves, whole plants such as vegetables, invertebrates such as ants, and vertebrates from fish to primates. No clear answer as to exactly what kind of death sin brought into the world exists, so perhaps different individuals can reasonably have different opinions.[10]

Human death, however, is a significant issue for all of us. While I worked for an oil company one summer, a Christian colleague asked me about the Adventist view of death. As I studied the Bible, I began to understand not only the Adventist position better, but also the reasonableness of other Christian beliefs. My friend noted that Jesus told Martha, "Everyone who lives and believes in me will never die" (John 11:26). He also noted that the Preacher seemed pretty depressed while writing Ecclesiastes and cautioned against interpreting every passage absolutely literally, including Ecclesiastes 9:5. Both of us learned from our Bible study. He recognized that the fires of hell don't burn into the infinite future, and I realized that life issues of the greatest importance don't have geometry-type proofs.

Evil Results for Humans

The results of Adam and Eve's bad choice in Genesis 3 are the loss of the blessings of Genesis 2. Their relationships had shattered. Listening to one of the creatures caused the loss of the couple's dominion over the whole of creation. Man's privilege of working the earth now became toil, and finally human beings would return to the dust. The woman's joy to be fruitful and multiply would now involve pain and subjection to her husband. The companionship and intimacy given to the couple in Genesis 2 degenerated into estrangement and shame. Humanity's free communion with God transformed itself into fear of His presence.

True human freedom for Adam and Eve meant the privilege of living with the consequences of choice—bad ones as well as good ones—and human dignity required accepting the responsibility.

Dealing With the Problem of Evil

Theodicy, defined as "a vindication of God's goodness and justice in the face of the existence of evil," attempts to explain logically the atrocities we see around us. If a God who is perfectly good and all-powerful exists, one would expect that evil should not exist. But since evil does exist, many conclude that either God does not exist, or is not perfectly good, or else is not all-powerful.[11]

Many atheists reject God because they so desperately want a caring and personal deity, and the world seems inconsistent with that picture.[12] Weinberg would like to find evidence in nature of a concerned Creator, but finds "sadness in doubting that we will."[13] Carl Sagan in his book *Contact* seems to want meaning, something more than naturalism. Thus as it turns out, evil presents a problem for atheists as well—how can there be such a thing as evil if the cosmos lacks a moral structure?[14]

Much has been written about the problem of evil.★ Perhaps the book that outlined the issues best for me was *Making Sense Out of Suffering,* by Peter Kreeft.[15] He begins by pointing out some easy answers that don't work: denying God's reality (atheism, demythologism, psychologism), denying God's power (polytheism, scientism, Zoroastrian dualism), denying God's goodness (satanism, pantheism, deism), or denying evil (Buddhism, Christian Science, theosophy).

Kreeft indicates that suffering is not a problem to conquer with answers, but a mystery to approach with the aid of clues to its ultimate significance, and for which the basic one is an attitude of humility. Inspiration provides the clue about the fall of Lucifer symbolized through the behavior of the ancient rulers of Babylon and Tyre (Isa. 14:4-20; Eze. 28:2-19). Ultimately, however, evil has no explanation—to explain it is to excuse it.

Inspiration clearly indicates that God is not the source of evil. Competition, survival of the fittest, the rule of tooth and claw, suffering, and death cannot be part of His ideal plan for development. He may use such methods from necessity (Rom. 8:28), but His employment of them as a preferred plan would conflict with how Scripture portrays His usual manner of working (Isa. 11:6; 65:25; Matt. 6:25-33; 10:29). Long past ages of suffering from evolutionary development would logically correlate with long future ages of suffering in hell. As Provonsha puts it, "to attribute the salient features of the theory of evolution to God is to come up with the wrong kind of God!"[16]

Free will gives the option for choice and thus opens up the possibility of evil. To prevent all evil, all freedom would have to be removed. Science fiction stories such as *The Matrix* are based on total control of humans by advanced computers, but it isn't a very appealing scenario. True free will includes the freedom to experience the consequences of free choice. God then lets the consequences work themselves out. Even though He doesn't remove the consequence when we make a bad choice, His grace makes possible a second chance for making good choices to redirect the results. Because of Simeon and Levi's evil choice at Shechem (Gen. 34:25-30) their descendants were cursed to live dispersed among the tribes of Israel (Gen. 49:7). However, when the Levites chose to take a stand against the apostasy at Sinai (Ex. 32:26-29), that scattering turned into a blessing as they became spiritual leaders throughout the land of Israel.[17]

Happiness is not synonymous with lack of suffering. It involves goodness and meaning, not just pleasure. God's love for us is too splendid to provide just mere happiness; love demands the perfecting of the beloved.[18] The velveteen rabbit* of the classic children's story learned that suffering makes you real.

The above explanations using free will and the benefits from suffering may answer some questions, but not the issue of fairness. Why do many generations benefit or suffer from the past choices of others, especially from Adam's original sin (Rom. 5:12; Ex. 20:5, 6)? Again, Kreeft provides some clues. Not only does he remind us that we are not so righteous ourselves (Isa. 64:6; Jer. 13:23), but he also forces us to consider something easily forgotten in our individualistic society. Each person has a solidarity with the rest of the human family, just as the individual church member is part of the body of Christ. Although I didn't win my daughter's scholarships, I am proud of them and am benefited by them. And though she is not responsible for my stupid jokes, she still gets embarrassed in front of her friends. We partake of the original sin of Adam, just as we can partake of the vicarious atonement of Christ (Rom. 5:15).

Even though we suffer for Adam's sin as part of the human lot, we can still ask why God couldn't just change the rules and not punish us. The problem with this solution is that there are different kinds of laws. Human-made laws are changeable at will. Physical laws set up by God can be superseded by miracles. However, some logical, mathematical, and metaphysical cause-and-effect laws even God can't change. Besides, who wants to let Hitler off the hook?

As finite human beings we look at the problem of evil within the constraints and limitations of time, but the real solution is yet in the future. The present life is but for a moment (Ps. 30:5; 2 Cor. 4:17) and is the birth pangs for an eternity of bliss. Suffering is not just a purposeless scandal, for there is something after this world.

Ultimately none of these explanations is totally satisfactory, for the answer to suffering is Someone, not something. At the end of the book of Job God gave Job Himself, not a well-thought-out answer, but Job was satisfied. Heaven is a person more than a place—and He is a person whom we can already experience here. We don't need to know why things happen as much as that someone cares and understands what we are going through. Love seeks not so much happiness as intimacy, so God does not isolate Himself from our pain.[19] My physicist friend from Moscow needed the personal touch of another who was hurting as she was, to know of Christ, who can "be touched with the feeling of our infirmities" (Heb. 4:15, KJV).

Antediluvians

Genesis 4 and 5 provide a brief glimpse, between the Fall and the Flood, of the results of evil and the promise of restoration. Chapter 4 parallels the previous chapter. Just as Adam and Eve experienced marital conflict, Cain and Abel's relationship breaks into sibling rivalry. And just as God questioned Adam, He now confronts Cain. The ground becomes part of a curse in both chapters 3 and 4, and just as Adam and Eve were banished, now the same happens to Cain.

John Steinbeck's *East of Eden*★ places the prototypical sibling rivalry of Cain and Abel in a modern setting. Steinbeck's Adam wants a Garden of Eden for his wife in central California. He thinks of naming his sons Cain and Abel, but eventually calls them Aron and Caleb (Cal). Sibling rivalry ensues. Aron is goodhearted and eventually withdraws into religious fervor to escape the world's corruption, whereas Cal becomes jealous of the favoritism shown to Aron. When Cal finds that his mother is a prostitute, he believes that her evil has passed down to him. He fears rejection, and his anger leads to revenge by telling Aron about their mother. The devastated Aron joins the Army and perishes in World War I, whereupon Cal becomes "marked with guilt." His hopelessness is countered when the family reads Genesis 4. Adam's housekeeper emphasized the Hebrew word *timshel* in verse 7 as giving a choice—"thou mayest conquer sin." Each person can choose their own moral destiny independent of the legacy of parents. Finally, on his deathbed Adam realizes that he must not crush his son with the unfairness of rejection, so he gives Cal his blessing with the single word *"Timshel!"*

Of Mice and Men, also by John Steinbeck, portrays the curses on Cain in terms of migratory agricultural workers in central California. The two main characters provide brotherly concern for each other, unlike most of the migrant laborers, who are not their "brother's keeper" but solitary wanderers like Cain. And just as Cain was cursed never to benefit from the fruits of his labor, the migrant workers lived an existence of economic futility. They wanted to recapture a paradise lost, but ultimately failed. However, it is possible for even the wanderer to find peace, for as Augustine prays, "You have made us for Yourself, and our hearts are restless until they find rest in You."

Genesis 4 continues the divine record of human history after Cain's banishment with the development of cultural innovations—urbanization by building a city, animal husbandry, the music of harp and flute, metal-working of bronze and iron, and even the poetry of Lamech. Those committed to God may find that they are not the only ones blessed with talents. Common grace benefits all, for God "makes his sun rise on the evil and on the good" (Matt. 5:45). This refutes the Manichean fallacy of two distinct groups in which only the righteous have truth.[20]

In the movie *Amadeus* Antonio Salieri unhappily finds this out in his relationship with Wolfgang Mozart. Salieri is the court musician dedicated to making music for God, but it is the frivolous Mozart who has received the gift of musical genius. God uses imperfect instruments to further His will: the Babylonians to punish Israel, Darwin to recognize variation in nature, geology to search for oil, and you and me to witness for Him.

Genesis 4 ends with Seth providing a new beginning. June Strong's *Song of Eve* gives one perception of antediluvian life.[21] The righteous lived in the mountains far from the lands of the wicked. One of the "sons of God" has married one of the "daughters of men," but still remembers his roots. The couple have a daughter who visits the gates of the Garden of Eden to worship, where she hears the mournful song of Eve and decides to follow God. She goes to live in the mountains with the righteous and eventually becomes the mother of Noah's wife. It is a sad and beautiful story.

Restoration

As human beings we have an innate feeling that there must be something better, that something has been lost. We recognize a law that we should practice but don't.[22] Sadly, we can't even live up to our own standards for ourselves.

In a materialistic worldview, hope for improvement comes through class struggle toward socialist utopianism (George Bernard Shaw), evolutionary progress and enlightenment (H. G. Wells), or freedom from repression and bondage to the subconscious (Sigmund Freud).[23] But Weinberg does not think "that science will ever provide the consolations that have been offered by religion in facing death."[24]

Rather than continual progress, however, the Bible worldview pictures a triad of creation, fall, and restoration.[25] The first Adam is created perfect, but possesses a fallen nature after sin. The Second Adam, though, makes possible a new nature. A perfect heaven and earth with the tree of life are despoiled by sin and finally destroyed (2 Peter 3:10-13), after which God makes all things new and restores the tree of life in the new earth (Rev. 22:2).

Genesis 3:15 promises victory over evil, and from there to Revelation 22 we find God's goal: "To restore in man the image of his Maker, to bring him back to the perfection in which he was created."[26] The sanctuary provides a tangible expression that God is doing something about evil. Nature shows the hope of new life each spring and that the horrors of war can be covered even at Antietam or Dachau. We may not say *"O felix culpa"*—"O fortunate fall"—for the loss is real, but the fall will be turned into an even closer unity with God.[27]

The morning after my dad's death many verses of hope kept going through my mind. While preparing to write this chapter, I looked through a book I once gave him: *The Jesus I Never Knew.* On the last page I found that he had written "Read 23 JAN '00." He died on February 5. That last page described a grandmother buried in a rural Louisiana cemetery. "In accordance with the grandmother's instructions, only one word is carved on the tombstone: 'Waiting.'"[28]

A Theological Perspective of Cain and Abel

In the story of Cain and Abel Bible students often focus on the contrasting ways the two brothers worshipped God. Usually we regard Abel as an example of someone recognizing his or her need for a Savior, and Cain as approaching religion through human works and efforts. We assume that Abel put his dependence on God and Cain on self. But the difference between them involves even more than that.

The Hebrew word for the two offerings is closely associated with the grain offering of Leviticus 2 and designates the brothers' offerings as "gifts." Apparently both of them brought them to express gratitude to God. But Cain had no real gratitude in his heart. Genesis 4:4, 5 declares that "the Lord had regard for Abel and his offering, but for Cain and his offering he had no regard." The offerings reflected the giver. Thus the real problem was not with Cain's offering but with Cain himself. The biblical account does not explicitly tell us what was wrong with him, but instead lets us watch him in action and from his resulting behavior figure out his problem ourselves. Cain murdered his brother. Murder is the taking of life, something that belongs only to God. Following the footsteps of his parents, Cain wanted to be like God. But would-be gods are self-centered. Unlike the true God, they do not care for others. And that was Cain's fundamental problem.

We observe his self-centeredness and arrogance in his response to God when He asked him, "Where is your brother Abel?" (Gen. 4:9). Cain replied, "I do not know; am I my brother's keeper?" (verse 9). The first murderer was indeed not his brother's keeper, though he should have been. Instead of accepting his brother and finding in Abel's relationship with God a model for both the human-human and divine-human relationships, Cain let his anger and rivalry grow into a raging beast that ruled his life.

God created human beings to care for each other just as He cares for all His creation. But sin always drives wedges between people. Those wedges or barriers can consist of jealousy, hate, blame, or an infinite list of other problems and motivations.

Cain was truly not his brother's keeper. He thought he needed no one. Even his relationship with God was superficial at best. But when the Lord told him that his punishment for his brother's murder was for Cain to be a wanderer, the man suddenly realized his need for community, including that with God. (He struggled with two overwhelming fears: the dread of his fellow humanity and the horror of being "hidden from your [God's] face" [verses 13, 14]). Although he had been alienated from both humanity and God for much of his life, he had not been aware of it until that moment. But that realization did not change him, as we observe in verses 23 and 24. Having left "the presence of the Lord" (verse 16) in more ways than one, he still had not learned what it truly meant to be his brother's keeper.

★ See p. 17.

[1] M. Shelley, *Frankenstein*, p. 42.

[2] *Ibid.*, p. 192.

[3] See also E. G. White, *Patriarchs and Prophets*, p. 54.

[4] *Ibid.*, pp. 54–56.

[5] Ian Plimer, *Telling Lies for God: Reason Versus Creationism* (Sydney, Australia: Random

House, 1994).

[6] Philip Yancey, *The Jesus I Never Knew* (Grand Rapids: Zondervan, 1995), pp. 69-80.

[7] *Ibid.,* p. 81.

[8] Stephen Jay Gould, *Ever Since Darwin: Reflections in Natural History* (New York: Norton, 1992), pp. 91-96.

[9] C. Ainsworth, "Life's Greatest Inventions," p. 32.

[10] Leonard Brand, "What Are the Limits of Death in Paradise?" *Journal of the Adventist Theological Society* 14, no. 1 (Spring 2003): 79.

[11] C. S. Lewis, *The Problem of Pain* (New York: Macmillan, 1962), p. 26.

[12] M. L'Engle, *Walking on Water,* p. 19.

[13] S. Weinberg, *Dreams of a Final Theory,* pp. 255, 256.

[14] Richard N. Ostling, "Protestant Philosopher at Notre Dame Carves Out Intellectual Room for God and Miracles," news release, Associated Press, Mar. 23, 2005.

[15] Peter Kreeft, *Making Sense Out of Suffering* (Ann Arbor, Mich.: Servant Books, 1986).

[16] J. W. Provonsha, *A Remnant in Crisis,* p. 75; Gen. 1-15.

[17] White, *Patriarchs and Prophets,* pp. 235, 236, 334, 350.

[18] Lewis, *The Problem of Pain,* pp. 40, 41, 46.

[19] White, *Education,* p. 263.

[20] M. A. Noll, *The Scandal of the Evangelical Mind,* p. 52.

[21] June Strong, *Song of Eve* (Hagerstown, Md.: Review and Herald Pub. Assn., 1987).

[22] C. S. Lewis, *Mere Christianity* (New York: Macmillan Pub. Co., 1952), p. 26.

[23] Yancey, *Soul Survivor,* p. 57.

[24] Weinberg, p. 260.

[25] Michael Edwards, *Towards a Christian Poetics* (Grand Rapids: William P. Eerdmans, 1984), p. 12.

[26] White, *Education,* p. 16; see also *Patriarchs and Prophets,* pp. 592-602.

[27] White, *The Desire of Ages,* p. 25.

[28] Yancey, *The Jesus I Never Knew,* p. 275.

5

Catastrophe

Genesis 6-9

In A.D. 79 Mount Vesuvius overwhelmed the inhabitants of Pompeii with 20 feet of ash, freezing in time a vignette of Roman life. Excavations reveal rutted streets, baths and brothels, villas and temples, amphitheaters and coliseums, and the casts of many fugitives who had perished in the disaster. Vesuvius and Pompeii provide often-used examples of the catastrophic forces of nature and the human tendency to be unprepared.

As I write, the Gulf Coast is reeling from Hurricane Katrina. The previous year a tsunami killed hundreds of thousands in Southeast Asia. Mount St. Helens caused widespread physical devastation in 1980.

In the 1920s J. Harlen Bretz theorized that catastrophic flooding* had eroded the deep gorges of the Pacific Northwest, but not until the 1960s did geologists generally accept his theory. They now believe that an ancient lake in Montana breached a glacial ice dam and that a volume of water equal to half of Lake Michigan swept across Washington State. The rushing water created mega-ripples, eroded the Columbia River gorge, and transported for miles boulders the size of houses.

Catastrophes are a well-accepted fact of life today, throughout history, and in the geologic record.* Many geologists attribute the extinction of the dinosaurs to a worldwide disaster triggered by a meteor impact off the Yucatan Peninsula in Mexico. Ancient mythologies from around the world record flood stories,* and this chapter will discuss Noah's flood as the prototypical disaster.

How many catastrophes have occurred over what time frame and how long ago?

We will first look at what science regards as evidence for uniformitarian geologic activity lasting billions of years. Next we will consider "short time" alternatives that attempt to fit all of the geologic column into a few thousand years, with most geologic activity occurring during Noah's unique one-year flood. Finding neither of these approaches satisfactory, we will summarize several intermediate models. Even then many unanswered questions will remain.

Standard Long-Age Geology

Discussion of long-age geology begins with a description of the three basic rock types and an outline of three organizing principles in geology: plate tectonics that explains rock types and locations, paleontology that deals with fossil types and locations, and radiometric dating that organizes it all sequentially. Following that, I will offer a few practical examples of the many geological time issues.★

Three Rock Types. Geological activity produces the spectacular natural scenery we observe on our planet: 1. Sedimentary—the Grand Canyon sedimentary rocks form vast horizontal layers of limestone, shale, sandstone, and conglomerate. Most sedimentary rocks are deposited by water with small clay particles settling out of still water to create shale layers and large pebbles forming into conglomerate layers as rapidly moving water slows and drops the load of material it is carrying. Sedimentary rocks often contain fossil material, such as coal, petrified wood, trilobites, and dinosaurs. 2. Igneous—volcanoes such as Mount Rainier, Mount Fuji, Mount Kilimanjaro, and large parts of the Andes developed from molten lava that erupted onto the earth's surface. Lava makes volcanic rocks, such as basalt, glassy obsidian, or lightweight pumice. Magma, liquid rock that doesn't reach the earth's surface, cools underground to become granitic-type rocks that make up much of such mountain ranges as the Sierra Nevada. 3. Metamorphic—intermediate pressures and temperatures have altered these rocks. Marble is metamorphosed limestone, and slate is metamorphosed shale. Parts of the Appalachian Mountains consist of metamorphic rocks. Igneous and metamorphic rocks often contain spectacular minerals. The Rocky Mountains, Alps, and Himalayas include all three rock types (as do the foundations of the New Jerusalem with its minerals of chalcedony, sapphire, emerald, and topaz [Rev. 21:19, 20]).

Plate Tectonics. Plate tectonic theory has brought many geological observations into a simple model of seven major moving crustal plates, most of them associated with a continent and the surrounding sea floor. The boundaries between such plates fall into three types: 1. At spreading centers the plates move apart. For example, along the Mid-Atlantic Ridge the oceanic crust forms, and on it the islands of Iceland, Surtsey, and the Azores. 2. Where the plates run into each other, the collision may build mountains, such as the Himalayas and Alps, or else one plate is subducted under (forced underneath) another, creating the Andes, the Japanese islands, and the Aleutian islands. This type of plate motion resulted in the recent Southeast Asia tsunami. 3. At transform faults, such as the San Andreas Fault in California, the plates slide past each other. The movement of the plates causes earthquakes.

The first suggestion that continents move came from theologians who correlated it with Noah's flood. Alfred Wegener presented his theory of continental drift in the early twentieth century, but most geologists did not accept it until the 1960s, when it finally caused a major scientific revolution. Although not a perfect model, the theory does explain volcanism and earthquakes, geologic and fossil matches between continents, the existence of tropical fossils in the polar regions, and direct evidence for continental movement of 2-15 centimeters per year. At the current rate of about 2 centimeters per year in the Atlantic Ocean, it would require 100 million years for the Old and New World to separate and reach their current positions. Creationist computer-modeling has simulated much more rapid plate motion, but it requires some rather unrealistic assumptions.[1]

Paleontology. The sedimentary geologic record, up to 10 miles thick in places, displays a general vertical sequence of fossils with progressively more complex organisms in the higher rocks—that is, fossils from single-celled organisms are the only ones to occur near the bottom, then organisms with shells, dinosaurs, mammals, and finally humans near the top. We do not find such things as the mixing of humans with dinosaurs or angiosperm pollen with trilobites.

Flood geology uses ecological zonation theory to explain the sequence. According to it, the Flood buried ocean-dwelling organisms first, then those living in low-lying swamps, and finally organisms dwelling at high elevations. In addition, mobile animals fleeing the rising floodwaters would get covered at higher elevations, and mammals and birds that float longer would get entombed higher in the geologic record than fish and amphibians that sink more quickly. This theory provides interesting ideas, but little research has been applied to specific situations. The sequence of fossil organisms displays no simple sorting of marine from terrestrial, or bottom dwellers from swimmers.

Radiometric Dates. The physical matter of the universe and earth appears to be old based on the agreement between various radiometric dating methods and the evidence for the constancy of the radioactive decay rates used in each method. Radiometric dates give ages for plate tectonic activity and the fossils that provide a working model that does amazingly well at explaining the sequence in the geologic record. My research in southern California has noted agreement between numerous of radiometric dates using several different methods.

Some who accept a short time frame discard the radiometric dates because of certain disagreements between different methods. Others accept radiometric ages of millions of years for the material in the rocks, but suggest that the constituent fossils did not get included in that ancient material until just the past few thousand years. Again, these interesting ideas have not been researched and provide little by way of a better explanation.

California Issues. In my geological studies I see plenty of evidence for time. The mountains along the west coast of the United States are mostly granitic-type rocks that formed beneath the earth's surface where liquid magma at more than 1112°F (600°C) cooled to a solid under 212°F (100°C). My geochemistry research focuses on these mountains of southern California, such as Mount San Jacinto, towering almost 11,000 feet above Palm Springs.

These mountains contain a sequence of fossils, layers of granite, rocks showing evidence of cooling, then more fossils. Standard estimates give a cooling time of millions of years. Cooling could have occurred in less time, but no calculations yet enable that massive a body of rock to get rid of its vast amount of heat during a one-year flood.

Practical Problems. Geologists find long time frame geology helpful in mineral and oil exploration. The concepts behind this paradigm give us principles to follow in making a more livable environment by improving groundwater quality, disposing of nuclear waste, minimizing soil and coastal erosion, managing and exploiting natural resources, and understanding climate change. Engineers find it useful in deciding how to mitigate the effect of such geohazards as volcanoes, earthquakes, tsunamis, and landslides. For example, policies for construction in southern California prohibit public facilities from being located on an active earthquake fault, defined to be "one that has ruptured in the past 11,000 years."[*] In a short-age model very few building sites would be available, including Loma Linda.

Christians would want to reject "infidel geology,"[2] but most geology is not of that type. How should we as Christians and citizens of this earth approach the practical results from current long-age geologic models? Although geologists recognize that these models are not totally correct, they are used until better models become available. If we employ the results from current models for practical purposes, will we eventually end up accepting the current model on which the results are based?

The astronomer Copernicus' book on heliocentric theory contains a preface by Andreas Osiander, who tried to save the geocentric system as fact by stating that the new heliocentric model was only for mathematical calculations. However, the simpler heliocentric system soon became the accepted picture, not just a calculational device.[3] If a model works, one comes to think it may be right.

Addressing Geology in a Short Time Frame

The long-age geologic data in the previous section do not harmonize well with a literal reading of Genesis 1-11. Such a reading depicts a fiat creation of everything a few thousand years ago. What kind of answers do young earth creationists give?

Life. The strongest evidence against a naturalistic origin for life comes from what seems to be intelligent design in the physical universe, the difficulty of explaining how life could develop at all, and the current range of discrete and complex organisms. None of these specifically addresses the issue of time, but they do demonstrate limits to naturalism.

Geology Data. Paraconformities—flat contacts between two different sedimentary layers deposited at different geological times—may offer the best evidence for a time frame shorter than billions of years. Although fossils in the two layers may seem to indicate the passage of tens of millions of years, lack of significant erosion between the two strata suggests that the successive layers were deposited in more rapid succession. At one such contact, easily seen from the rim of the Grand Canyon, tens of millions of years are supposedly missing.[4]

Creationists have done research related to several geological time issues. For example, a number of Adventist scientists have studied the Yellowstone fossil forests during the past 40 years.★ Initially it seemed that the dozens of layers of upright petrified trees indicated that dozens of forests had sequentially grown and been buried over tens of thousands of years. Ensuing studies of the upright trees have suggested, however, that they are probably not in position of growth, but were transported before burial. A standard geology reference now uses such a transport model.[5]

History and Philosophy of Science. Creationists give several generic answers to the time issues: 1. Many more scientists are studying nature from a long-age perspective, so one would expect them to have more answers. 2. Science has made plenty of mistakes and has unanswered problems. However, it may be logically inconsistent to emphasize the limitations of science, but still use it to support a creation/flood model.

But no matter which side of the issue we stand on, we must always be careful how we extrapolate from scientific data. 3. A Christian oil geologist I interviewed with for a job first pointed out to me the dangers inherent whenever we extrapolate from what we observe. Let me give a simple illustration. As a good scientist, I have measured my daughter's height and plotted it through the years. By extending that increase in height into the future, I find that she will be 9 feet tall when she reaches age 30. Fortunately that extrapolation is not valid. Extrapolation back in time from a few thousand years of recorded scientific data and history to the billions of years for the age of the earth has scientific support, but extrapolation from years to millions of years still requires caution.

4. Revolutions in scientific understandings have happened in the past, as explored in Thomas Kuhn's classic 1970 book, *The Structure of Scientific Revolutions*. We have already discussed the paradigm shifts resulting from Wegener's theory of continental drift, Bretz's theory of catastrophic flooding in the Pacific Northwest, and meteorite impacts destroying the dinosaurs. Some creationists hope for a future scientific revolution that will confirm a short time frame.

Conversely, Adventist perspectives about geology have undergone their own revolution since the time of George McCready Price, the Adventist father of modern creationism.[6] We have recognized that glaciation has occurred, that dinosaurs really existed, and that the fossil record displays order. Many accept the evidence of great age for the universe, the solar system, and the inorganic matter of the earth.

5. Circumstances affect our perception of time. Einstein said, "When a man sits with a pretty girl for an hour, it seems like a minute. But let him sit on a hot stove for a minute and it's longer than any hour. That's relativity."[7] Relativistic effects have been suggested for solving the time discrepancy between Genesis and science.[8] Lewis's *Chronicles of Narnia* give a fictional representation of such disparate relative time frames: children disappear from England for a few moments, but live for years in Narnia while gone.

6. In the past, theists have often "explained" natural phenomena by appealing to God's inscrutable ways. As science learned more, less needed to be explained by a God filling in gaps in our knowledge. Now time may

be a similar God-of-the-gaps argument for evolution, since it assumes that given enough time anything can happen. The impossible becomes possible, and the possible probable.[9] As Lewis Carroll's queen said to Alice: "Sometimes I've believed as many as six impossible things before breakfast." But although the God-of-the-gaps argument has fallen into disrepute, theists still recognize the possibility for direct divine intervention.

The Supernatural. Although creationists may have no alternative model to replace the long-age model, perhaps it is because "our heavenly Father has a thousand ways"[10] of which we know nothing. The nonrepeatable creation events required divine intervention, something difficult to study by the scientific method. The Flood too apparently involved more than natural causes.[11]

Words of Caution. Some creationists have used poor geological arguments to support a short time frame, but even the few good arguments present a problem. Those who believe that the limited data consistent with a short-age model makes it a defensible scientific model can easily be unprepared for studying geology. The arguments such individuals employ are usually ad hoc, theoretical arguments to defend the Bible, but they present no useful working alternative model that will better explain my own or other geology research.

Let us examine this danger more carefully. One must keep in mind: 1. Short-age arguments and models based on partial data can be quite convincing without being correct. 2. Evidence for rapid, widespread activity can easily fit into a long-age model. 3. Problems with one particular long-age theory do not necessarily mean that a short-age model is required. 4. For significant data no short-age explanation is available. 5. No comprehensive short-age model is even available to rival the standard long-age model. 6. Ultimately, any biblical model would include some supernatural activity, immediately making it incompatible with naturalistic science. Could it be possible that in our attempts to explain the Flood scientifically we could be leaving God out of the picture? If we found a scientific model to explain the Flood, would those who refuse to accept it just argue that it shows that we do not need divine intervention at all?

One should not base a belief in Scripture on scientific evidence, because that puts science above the Bible and reason and sense perception above revelation, tempting us to discard the Bible when the scientific evidence is found to be incompatible with our understanding of Scripture.

Scientific Models

Finding neither the long-time nor the short-time models completely satisfactory, we now summarize several intermediate approaches used to harmonize nature and inspiration. Multiple working hypotheses and knowing the pros and cons of each model will aid our attempt to be more objective. These intermediate models are good faith attempts to find an intellectually appealing model of origins that takes both the Bible and scientific data seriously. For completeness we include two extreme approaches as well.

Entire Universe Young. Many young earth creationists accept the idea of the entire universe being only a few thousand years old. This model uses the most literal reading of Scripture, but fits poorly with much scientific evidence.★

Young Life, Old Universe and Earth. The passive gap theory accepts that other worlds were inhabited and that the earth's matter may have existed before Creation week (Job 1:6; 38:7).[12] The Genesis 1 creation of the heavens includes only the atmosphere and of the earth includes only the dry land. The *Adventist Review* has suggested this view on various occasions,★ and it is a common understanding held by Adventists. This model helps explain some astronomical observations and radiometric dates.

However, this view is not inherently obvious from the biblical account, because inspired records suggest that God created the physical matter by fiat at the same time as He did the earth's life forms (Ps. 33:6, 9).[13] The Sabbath commandment appears to commemorate God's creation of everything in seven days. This model is not scientifically helpful if it rejects rain, catastrophes, and plate tectonics with its attendant volcanism, earthquakes, and mountain building before Creation week. In fact, this model leaves little happening for the first half of Creation Week, since any activity then was merely a modification of hydrologic, geologic, and astronomical cycles that had already existed for millions of years.

Young Life, but Not Exactly 6,000 Years Old nor All Geology in One Year. Various Old Testament manuscripts give different lengths of time for the genealogies between Adam and Abraham.[14] Tens of thousands of years would remove many problems with archaeology, radiocarbon dating, and the ice ages. Such a model spreads out much of the geological activity across thousands of years and allows time for the migration, ecologic succession, and speciation of living organisms.

A Seven-Day Creation and a Local Flood, but Life Before the Genesis Creation. In this active gap theory, the fossil record results from a long period of life destroyed before the Genesis creation (of perhaps only the

Garden of Eden). Relativistic effects might be included, and death in the fossil record could be the result of the devil's sin.[15]

These ideas have not been developed scientifically and have several difficulties. Why would previous life be so similar to that of a recent creation? The Bible indicates that death resulted from Adam's sin (Rom. 5:12) and it assumes a worldwide Flood (1 Peter 3:20; 2 Peter 2:5; 3:6). Migration would have been easier than an ark to save life from a local flood. Also, many local floods have occurred throughout history, so God's promise not to destroy the earth again with a flood (Gen. 8:21; 9:11) must mean that it was more than local.

God as Creator, but Working During Long Time Periods. Many evangelical Christian scientists support progressive creation or theistic evolution. These models accept the standard scientific interpretation of long ages for the geologic data, while acknowledging God as Creator and designer. However, they also postulate death before sin.[16]

Totally Naturalistic. The standard scientific model assumes that we can explain everything in terms that humans can understand and control. However, life and its design seem difficult to explain naturalistically.

Conclusion. As can be seen, no perfect harmonization of science and Scripture yet exists. It is as difficult to stretch biblical teaching into a long time frame as it is to fit geology into a short time frame. Both can be forced, but neither flows naturally from the data. Some intermediate scenario is more realistic than either of the extremes. However, I am not smart enough to figure out just how God acted in history. Reality probably includes some combination of the models listed, but goes beyond them, just as the elephant is more than what each of the six blind men of Hindustan* could visualize. Any model must be honest with both scientific data and Scripture, with the realization that a seven-day Creation week is important but unverifiable scientifically. Gamaliel's counsel (Acts 5:38, 39) is apropos: true ideas will prosper and false ideas disappear independent of church action.

As I develop my understanding of origins, it includes not only reason based on evidence from both nature and Scripture, but also faith in a loving, omniscient, and eternal God. Any origins model that misrepresents God's character or that puts human reason above God's revelation is unacceptable.

Destruction and Re-creation

At Creation God conquered the watery chaos by bringing order. On the second day He set the dome of the firmament as a barrier to the waters above, and on the third day He established the dry land as a barrier to the seas. But the Flood waters broke those barriers from both above and beneath (Gen. 7:11, KJV), and the earth returned to primeval chaos. It was such a catastrophe that even the devil feared for his life.[17]

With the destruction at its height in the center of the Flood story, "God remembered" (Gen. 8:1) and once again brought order out of chaos (cf. Jer. 4:23).[18] The wind or spirit moved on the water, the waters receded, and the dry land emerged. (Scripture depicts God conquering the watery chaos in smaller ways at the parting of the Red Sea and the Jordan River and when Jesus walked on the stormy billows and stilled the storm.)

The Flood raises an issue that disturbs us. How can God be fair in a world that seems so chaotic? After all, the Flood destroyed the idea that only predictable things will happen. To a certain extent we have gotten somewhat used to that fact. We can tolerate certainty occasionally mixed with surprises. Many popular games operate on strategy plus random chance, so that winning depends on skill plus luck. But we want things as predictable as possible—including God. But as C. S. Lewis said about the Christ character Aslan in his Narnia series, he was "not a tame lion." We cannot always predict what God might do. He can surprise us, as He did those who lived before the Flood when He swept the earth clean of the evil they had caused. Fortunately for us, while the Lord of the Bible is just and fair, He is also merciful. We cannot always determine beforehand how He will respond, but we can know that it will always be out of love.

The natural world also can operate the same way. Law and order make science possible, but complexity theory and quantum mechanics indicate that determinism can never completely explain the world around us.

Determinism and Uncertainty in Science. Science once believed nature to be totally deterministic. Astronomers used Newton's laws of gravitation to predict the return of Halley's Comet in 1758-1759. Pierre Simon de Laplace went so far as to suggest that the future behavior of the universe was absolutely predictable if only we knew the present positions and forces for all particles in it.

Complexity theory, however, recognizes many situations that are far too difficult for us to trace every effect to its cause. Complexity or chaos results from slight imprecisions in initial conditions, thus totally changing the final results. In addition, the Heisenberg uncertainty principle of quantum mechanics indicates that because atomic particles also behave as waves, we cannot know exactly both the position and speed of a particle at the same time. Thus determinism, which once had seemed a fundamental principle of science, can no longer fully describe all reality.

Order and Chaos in the Natural World. God granted the first couple dominion over the creation, but human relations with the world deteriorated after the curses at the Fall and the Flood. Animals would live in fear of humans, and people could now use animals for food (Gen. 9:2, 3). Natural disasters such as the Flood may be direct "acts of God" as a result of sin, but many others may also occur independent of any human evil (Luke 13:4, 5).

Justice and Brokenness in Human Relations. Human beings want certainty, fairness, and justice in their various relationships. Scripture (Ps. 73; Prov. 4:18; Eccl. 5:8; 7:15; 8:14; Isa. 59:4, 9, 14; Micah 6:8) and secular literature frequently discuss this theme. After sin humanity wanted to reconnect the relationship between earth and heaven that sin had broken. Enoch prophesied of a reunion of earth and heaven (Jude 14, 15), and God broke the barrier between them when He took Enoch to heaven. Then Jesus forever shattered the barrier by becoming human and taking that human form to heaven. But He did it from another aspect of His divine personality.

God's Judgment and Grace. God's justice is a major theme in Scripture (Ps. 89:14; Rev. 15:3). The Flood resulted from His just judgment, whereas in other Near Eastern mythologies capricious gods send the disaster on a whim.[19]

The judgment at the Flood is a warning for the final judgment (Matt. 24:37-39; 2 Peter 3:6, 7), also a fair judgment that will take into account our circumstances (Ps. 87:6; Rom. 2:14). The final judgment will display God's fairness to heavenly beings, the righteous, and the wicked. In the Flood we also see God's mercy. He is pained (Gen. 6:6) and suffers, but is also gracious.[20] Although the Flood was a judgment, the ark provided salvation for those who accepted it. God made a covenant promise with this remnant both before and after the Flood (Gen. 6:18; 9:9-17), sealing it with a rainbow mimicking the dome-shaped firmament as a barrier to the waters above.[21]

Before the Flood God sees humanity's evil and destroys it (Gen. 6:5-7), while after the Flood He sees humanity's evil and preserves (Gen. 8:21).[22] At the first Advent the unfallen worlds expected God to destroy as He did at the flood, but instead He sent His "embassage of divine grace."[23] In Isaiah God summarizes His graciousness by remembering His promise to Noah to be angry no longer: "my kindness shall not depart from thee, neither shall the covenant of my peace be removed" (Isa. 54:10, KJV).

A Theological Perspective on the Flood

Seven days after God directed Noah and his family to board the ark (Gen. 7:1) the Flood burst upon the earth. Earlier in Genesis 1 God had created the world out of chaos and declared it good. But in Genesis 7 He "de-created" it because evil had plunged it into an even worse type of chaos. The biblical narrator describes the events of the Flood in a way that mirrors in reverse order what happened during Creation week. Genesis 1:6-8 has God separating the waters above from the waters below. But in Genesis 7:11 they rush together again. Dry land emerged in Genesis 1:9, 10, and now vanishes in Genesis 7:19, 20. The living things He had joyously created in Genesis 1:20-26 He sadly blotted out in Genesis 7:21-23. The good creation that sin had corrupted was no more. Only Noah and his family remained (Gen. 7:23).

But the story does not end with a return to primeval chaos. God "remembered" Noah (Gen. 8:1). Whenever God "remembers" in Scripture He then intervenes in human lives and history. For example, He rescued Lot from Sodom (Gen. 19:29), gave Rachel children (Gen. 30:22), and freed Israel from Egyptian bondage (Ex. 2:24; 6:6).

Here the remembering leads to the re-creation of the earth. As the Lord does so, He follows the same sequence of Genesis 1. A wind blows (Gen. 8:1; cf. Gen. 1:2), the fountains of the deep and the windows of heaven close (Gen. 8:2; cf. Gen. 1:6), the waters recede (Gen. 8:3; cf. Gen. 1:9, 10), and the dove returns with an olive leaf (Gen. 8:11; cf. Gen. 1:11, 12). After the ark comes to rest on dry ground, God allows the saved animals and human beings to leave it and be fruitful and multiply (Gen. 8:15-19; cf. Gen. 1:21-28).

God does not need to re-create the sun, moon, and stars, but He does mention them in Genesis 8:22. Because the Flood account parallels what has gone before, it suggests that the biblical author intends the strange incident in Genesis 9:20-27 to act as a counterpart to Genesis 3. In both of them human beings get themselves into trouble because of fruit growing in a garden (the Garden of Eden/a vineyard) and God has to put a curse on those involved. In addition, the vineyard story answers the question If God re-created the world, why do we find evil in it again?

★ See p. 17.

---

[1] John R. Baumgardner and Michael J. Oard, "Forum on Catastrophic Plate Tectonics," *TJ* 16, no 1 (2002): 57-85.

[2] See Ellen G. White, *Spiritual Gifts* (Battle Creek, Mich.: Steam Press, 1864), vol. 3, p. 91; *Patriarchs and Prophets,* p. 112.

[3] Charles E. Hummel, *The Galileo Connection: Resolving Conflicts Between Science and the Bible* (Downers Grove, Ill.: InterVarsity Press, 1986), pp. 48, 49.

[4] Ariel A. Roth, "Those Gaps in the Sedimentary Layers," *Origins* 15 (1988): 75-92.

[5] William J. Fritz, *Roadside Geology of the Yellowstone Country* (Missoula, Mont.: Mountain Press, 1985).

[6] James L. Hayward, "Shifting Views of the Past: Adventists and the Historical

Sciences," *Spectrum* 28, no. 1 (Winter 2000): 65-68.

[7] Steve Mirsky, "Einstein's Hot Time," *Scientific American* 287, no. 3 (September 2002): 102.

[8] Gerald L. Schroeder, *The Science of God: The Convergence of Scientific and Biblical Wisdom* (New York: Free Press, 1997): S. Clark Rowland, "Space Odysseys and Time Dilation," *Spectrum* 29, no. 1 (2001): 30, 31.

[9] George Wald, "The Origin of Life," *Scientific American* 191, no. 2 (August 1954): 48.

[10] White, *The Desire of Ages,* p. 330.

[11] White, *Patriarchs and Prophets,* p. 119.

[12] White, *The Desire of Ages,* p. 834; *Patriarchs and Prophets,* pp. 41, 42; *The Great Controversy* (Mountain View, Calif.: Pacific Press Pub. Assn., 1911), p. 497; *The Story of Redemption* (Washington, D.C.: Review and Herald Pub. Assn., 1947), p. 19.

[13] White, *Patriarchs and Prophets,* p. 45; *The Desire of Ages,* p. 20.

[14] Gerhard F. Hasel, "Genesis 5 and 11: Chronogenealogies in the Biblical History of Beginnings," *Origins* 7, no. 1 (1980): 23-37.★

[15] Gary Chartier, "Jack Provonsha on Fundamentalist Geology: 'More Needs to Be Said,'" La Sierra *Criterion,* Nov. 8, 1985, pp. 1, 4, 8.

[16] L. James Gibson, "Biblical Creation: Is There a Better Model?" *Ministry,* May 2000, pp. 5-8.

[17] White, *Patriarchs and Prophets,* p. 99.

[18] L. Turner, *Back to the Present,* pp. 83, 84.

[19] *Ibid.,* pp. 81, 82.

[20] David Atkinson, *The Message of Genesis 1-11* (Downers Grove, Ill.: InterVarsity Press, 1990), pp. 136, 137.

[21] Laurence A. Turner, *Genesis* (New York: Continuum, 2000), p. 53.

[22] *Ibid.,* p. 51.

[23] White, *The Desire of Ages,* p. 37.

6

A Search for Certainty
Genesis 9:18-11:26

I want certainty and like perfection, from balancing a budget to solving a physics problem correctly. My wife says I'm obsessive-compulsive. As a high school freshman I wrote an English essay explaining that math was my favorite subject because it "has only one correct answer." In college I majored in physics and math, because I didn't like the ambiguity of the humanities or people relations. Because I also enjoy the outdoors, I pursued a master's degree in geology—but it wasn't quantitative. Then, while taking a geology field mapping class, I learned to speculate about ambiguous scientific models to get an A grade on geologic reports. Three years of that ambiguity were enough, and I went back to being a social recluse—15 years of research in nuclear physics in which some of the constants are accurate to eight significant figures. Finally, I am doing geology again after coming to accept that uncertainty is a part of life.

People in Genesis 1-11 also go through cycles, have difficulty with relationships, develop pride in their knowledge, want to make a name for themselves, and crave certainty. Although the genealogies display the interconnectedness of human relationships (Acts 17:26), brokenness returns to the world through Noah's immediate family and extends to all with the confusion of language at Babel.

The Babel builders wanted knowledge, certainty, control, and autonomy, just as Eve did. They sought to reach to heaven for fame, for safety from another deluge, and to determine the cause of the flood.[1] But their compulsion resulted only in chaos, leading to the confusion of language, broken relationships, and the isolation of people from each other.

Language. Early in the twentieth century the philosopher Ludwig Wittgenstein recognized that language is ambiguous because it is not private—it derives its meaning from relationships in communities where words take on specific meanings.[2] Consider the jargon you use in your professional, church, sports, or any other kind of group. As a result, language plays a major role in our perceptions and how we think about the world.[3] Because language uses metaphor and embraces multiplicity of meaning and paradox, it enables us to tell jokes and write poetry.* On the other hand, it can be frustrating when we want to describe things unambiguously.

Restoration. Out of the chaos at Babel, God brings restoration by calling Abram. Although the ground had been cursed, Cain made a wanderer, and the Babel builders scattered, Abram's descendants will inherit the Promised Land. The Lord will build them a city, and they will be a blessing to all (Gen. 12:2; 15:7; Heb. 11:10). The Nephilim, Nimrod, and the builders of Babel attempted to make a name for themselves, but God gave Abram a new name that would become great (Gen. 12:2).

Christ brings the ultimate restoration of what humanity lost in the first chapters of Genesis. That restoration is by blood better than that of Abel (Heb. 12:24). Christ sets aside Lamech's law of retaliation (Gen. 4:24; Matt. 5:38, 39); takes upon Himself our alienation from God (Mark 15:34); and bears the curse (Gal. 3:13, 14). He seals the covenant (Matt. 26:28) of Noah and restores our relationship with God (Rom. 8:14-16). Our Savior will give pure speech, so all may serve with one accord (Zeph. 3:9) and hear in their own tongue (Acts 2:8-11). Through Him we will once again bear the divine image (2 Peter 1:4).[4]

This chapter will describe our search for knowledge and certainty and discuss limits to what we may be able to find. Suggestions for dealing with uncertainty will center on "third options" rather than either of two extreme positions. For dealing with interpersonal relationships the emphasis will be on winning people instead of arguments. Ultimately, one can believe and act without having all the answers.

Knowledge

Humanity's use of the supernatural to explain the events and processes of nature has decreased over time. In Bible times people saw God as the direct cause for weather, health, and infertility. Because early scientists did so well at explaining how God works in the physical sciences, later generations extended their methods to more and more features in biology—how the body works, how species change, and where life itself comes from. Eventually many felt that God's direct agency was no longer needed at all. Although divine purposeful design might be a primary explanation of "why," the Western mind excluded it from science that deals with the secondary explanations of "how." Thus teleology, or ultimate purpose as an explanation, fell into disrepute.

Scientific Method. The modern world has come to see the scientific method as the best way to arrive at truth. It uses sensory perception, experimentation, human reason, and logic, rather than supernatural revelation. Seeking to be *objective,* it attempts to operate independent of the observer and their biases. And its *reductionism* assumes the whole to be no more than the sum of the parts. The scientific method assumes a *naturalistic* and a *deterministic* world, in which every effect has a natural cause. Furthermore, it requires a *uniformitarian* world that one can analyze for *repeatable* events in order to make *predictions* about future events and *test* them. Summarizing, science postulates a mechanistic universe.

We all want what science offers—control over our lives and environment and a predictable existence. Scientifically tested skin creams, hair coloring, eyeglasses, immunizations, antibiotics, and anesthesia put us in charge of our bodies. Indoor light bulbs, heating, and air-conditioning enable us to manage our environment. And CD players, radios, and movies help us regulate our emotions.

Science gives us more leisure time by providing the convenience of cars and airplanes, photocopiers, and calculators and computers. Lightning rods avert what used to be regarded as God's judgments. We can thank physics, chemistry, and biology for these advances and geology for finding the natural resources to build them and the oil and coal to run them.

God's Interaction With the Creation. How then does the modern scientific mind-set understand God's interaction with nature? Weinberg argues that the only way "any sort of science can proceed is to assume that there is no divine intervention." Science and religion are incompatible, for religion arose "in the hearts of those who longed for the continual intervention of an interested God."[5]

It is as difficult to understand the divine-human interaction in the natural world as in the Bible's inspiration and in Jesus' incarnation. One explanation sees God as the primary agent who set up nature's laws as secondary agents to do His will, and in so doing He limited Himself.

Once He has put good natural laws in place, God does not usually intervene directly. He can work through the laws of medical science to provide healing and the laws of agricultural science to give us food. Thus we thank God as the primary source and the physician or farmer as the secondary agent. We can explain even the parting of the Jordan and death from eating quails as God using natural laws serendipitously.

When God does intervene, it is minimal because He is not capricious. Miracles may break petty rules but still follow a higher order: normal processes merely speeding up (water to wine, feeding 5,000, healing) or as an insight on how the perfect creation should operate (stilling the storm, resurrection).[6]

Major interventions such as design at Creation and destruction at the Flood are unique occurrences that can be true without necessarily being amenable to scientific study, i.e., explainable in naturalistic terms.

Knowledge Sources. Francis Bacon introduced the concept of nature and revelation as God's two books,* and a quote to that effect appears opposite the title page of Darwin's *Origin of Species*.* Science is the human interpretation of God's creation as marred by sin, whereas theology is the human interpretation of God's revelation through human channels. Both science and theology requires a blend of faith and reason.

We could expand the "two books" to include the senses, reason, and the Holy Spirit. Loving God with the whole mind (Matt. 22:37) means searching for truth through all these sources. The Christian depends primarily on Scripture and the guidance of the Holy Spirit, but does so in conjunction with the methods of science: the empirical method that uses the senses and rational inquiry that uses reason. Human beings have employed all these knowledge sources to support Christianity.[7] Jesus provided evidence, although not the signs or proof the Jews demanded, nor the wisdom and reason that the Greeks desired (Matt. 12:38-40; 1 Cor. 1:22-24).

How can we balance both knowledge from nature and revelation? On the one hand, we use knowledge from science instead of revelation to explain the earth's motion, to clean the fungus in a house (Lev. 14:49-53), and to explain sickness as the result of genes or a bad lifestyle rather than a direct curse from God. On the other hand, we are warned of trusting the senses and human reason over revelation, as Eve did at the tree of knowledge. Satan's final deceptions will appeal to the senses: power, signs, and deceptive wonders (2 Thess. 2:9), fire from heaven (Rev. 13:13), or an angel of light (2 Cor. 11:14; Gal. 1:8). Unfortunately, conflict between knowledge from science and from theology produces uncertainty.

Uncertainty, Paradoxes, and Conflict

Human beings want certainty, but uncertainty is an inescapable part of life. Miguel de Unamuno said, "Those who believe that they believe in God, but without passion in their hearts, without anguish in mind, without uncertainty, without doubt, and even at times without an element of despair, believe only in the idea of God, and not in God Himself."[8] Self-assured, dogmatic teachers with an air of infallibility attract those who want certainty, but such individuals have little impact on somebody looking for genuine scholarship.[9]

Scientific Uncertainty. Modern science has its own vagueness and ambiguity.[10] Intuition cannot picture nature under the extreme conditions that the new physics describes to us as we explore it with the theories of relativity, quantum mechanics, complexity theory, and astrophysics. These theories indicate that objectivity and determinism, some of the traditional foundations of science, are not absolute. Niels Bohr, one of the architects of quantum mechanics, recognized a paradox: For simple truths, an opposite statement cannot be defended, but for the "deep truths" an opposite statement also contains a deep truth.[11]

Paradoxes. Humanity has wrestled with various paradoxes for millennia. For example, in the Liar's Paradox, Eubulides asks, "Does a man who says he is now lying speak the truth?"[12] Some pairs of sayings can be paradoxical, such as "Look before you leap" versus "He who hesitates is lost." Latching on to one part of a paradoxical truth and ignoring the rest takes an extreme position as the whole truth.

Christians have also struggled with such paradoxes as Christ being both Creator and creature;[13] predestination and free will; justice and mercy; and faith and works. In Christ's day His people had to deal with the paradox of a conquering king versus a suffering servant (e.g., Isa. 52; 53). Scripture makes statements that defy human logic: rest under a yoke (Matt. 11:28-30); the last shall be first (Matt. 20:16); the humble are exalted (Matt. 23:12; Luke 9:48); and power in weakness (2 Cor. 12:9). Only in Christ are some of the paradoxes resolved (e.g., mercy cannot be divorced from truth and justice; the righteousness of the law is not an enemy to peace [Ps. 85:10]).[14]

Science and Religion Conflict. The science and religion conflict, so frequently in the news, comes from putting the creature above the Creator. To remind His people of that fact in the Old Testament, God directed the plagues on the Egyptians against the nature gods of cattle, sun, and Nile. The three and a half years of drought in Elijah's time showed the impotence of Baal, the god of weather and fertility (1 Kings 18).

The Sadducees, the "scientists" of Jesus' day, rejected divine power and tried to explain divine mysteries in human terms.[15] Jesus charged them as not knowing God's power because they disbelieved in the resurrection (Matt. 22:23-33; Acts 23:8). (Interestingly, the intensely religious Pharisees received the most withering criticism from Jesus [Matt. 23].)

The Galileo affair may be the most dramatic historical example of conflict. Many in the sixteenth-century church believed that the earth held a central but fallen place in God's creation, in contrast to the perfect and unchanging celestial bodies around the earth. Galileo used his telescope to find sunspots, craters on the moon, and moons orbiting the planet Jupiter. To some, his observations indicated imperfections in the celestial bodies and that the earth was not the unique center, so the pope, to satisfy a vocal faction, had to allow the church to condemn Galileo's ideas. (The church administrator who oversaw Galileo's censure was quite knowledgeable about astronomy and reduced the punishment to house arrest.) Galileo himself was not without fault. His sarcasm made enemies, and his book made the pope appear a fool. In addition, his science had problems as well, with its use of astrology, rejection of elliptic orbits, and overstatement of his case.

Thomas Aquinas, who synthesized theology with the geocentric worldview of Ptolemy and Aristotle, had set the stage for the conflict. Aquinas believed that reason and revelation should be consistent since they have the same Author. Because he had united theology with a particular scientific model, it made Galileo's arguments against the geocentric model appear to undermine the Bible as well. The entire incident warns us not to tie theology to a specific scientific model.

As for the current conflict between science and religion, Andrew Dickson White's 1896 book, *History of the Warfare of Science With Theology in Christendom,* set the tone for it. He portrayed religion as obstructing the progress of scientific truth. (Many historians of science now question the book's whole premise.)

Others see science as the culprit. Bryan Appleyard's 1994 book, *Understanding the Present: Science and the Soul of Modern Man,* views the whole scientific enterprise as being in opposition to the human spirit. Václav Havel, a poet and playwright and one-time president of the Czech Republic, included in science's dangers to civilization mass television, the population explosion resulting from advances in health care, and environmental destruction produced by our craving for material goods.

The human fear of technology and mutant science is illustrated by the ancient myth of Prometheus, who gave fire and words to humans, and more recently in Frankenstein's monster and in the computer HAL of *2001: A Space Odyssey.*

Reasons for Uncertainty, Paradox, and Conflict. Several reasons for the current situation are possible. Some methods of acquiring knowledge are simply better not to use, such as Eve's search for the knowledge of good and evil. Or the complete picture may be too confusing. For the Israelites, their single supernatural being enabled them to combat the surrounding polytheistic religions. But in the process the Old Testament portrays evil as coming from God instead of Satan.

Inspired statements may have multiple explanations. The "virgin shall conceive" of Isaiah 7:14, KJV, had several fulfillments.[16] The Old Testament mingles the events of Christ's first and second advents. Matthew 24 combines predictions of both the destruction of Jerusalem and the end of the world. Adventists seem comfortable with more than one creation event in Genesis 1, and the Flood involving events beyond a single year. Also we see multiple interpretations of one set of data illustrated by the familiar rabbit/duck or the young/old woman optical illusions.*

Perhaps part of our problem is that we have been asking the wrong questions. I would not want to answer either yes or no to the question "Have you stopped beating your wife?" Answers are available for origins questions, but often not to the questions that we actually ask. Because the Jews had the wrong expectations about the Messiah in Jesus' day, they didn't get the answers they wanted. Jesus forbade the disciples to announce that He was the Messiah,[17] because the Jews had such a misconception of the Messiah's role. Even the resurrection was not enough of an answer, as Jesus explained in the parable of the rich man and Lazarus (Luke 16:31).

As I have previously stated in these chapters, I have not attempted to give "the one right answer," but to provide evidence so that readers can decide for themselves. Some of the options have been deliberately "outside the box." For a visual example, think of drawing four connected straight lines through nine dots set in a square. The solution involves thinking outside the box, i.e., drawing lines that extend outside the box formed by the nine dots.

Perhaps God, in order to keep us humble, doesn't give us all the answers. People who "know all the answers" can be unpleasant to live with.

Ultimately the answer to the issue of origins is not just facts, but a Person. Jesus is "the way, the truth, and the life" (John 14:6, KJV). The philosopher Michael Polanyi has suggested that all knowledge is personal, that there is no such thing as a wholly objective detached scientific understanding.[18]

Leap of Faith. God gives sufficient answers, but never absolute proofs. Room for doubt always remains,[19] so belief in God requires a leap of faith, as Sören Kierkegaard recognized.[20] It was such a leap that the famous middle-aged astronomer Allan Sandage was willing to take.[21] G. K. Chesterton observed that people can find truth with logic only if they have already found truth without it. Anselm described the process as "faith seeking understanding."*

Solutions

Nature[22] and science[23] can be compatible with inspiration. Paul seems to approve of the scientific method when he comments, "Test everything; hold fast to what is good" (1 Thess. 5:21). Conflict dwindles in significance when the study of nature's complexities points to a Creator bigger than we are and infinite in wisdom.

Third Options. We would like to accept the evidence from revelation and the evidence from nature and to have compatibility between them. Unfortunately, the naturalist soon gives up on revelation and the "supernaturalist" on nature. Might there be a third option? We could put aside the search for compatibility for now. Instead, accepting both revelation and nature, we will be willing to take as long as it needs to work toward compatibility. Above all, we must emphasize honesty over coherence and easy solutions.

The miracle of the disciples' catch of fish provides an example. It made no sense to fish during the day, so the disciples had several options: 1. Disbelieve what didn't make sense and refuse to obey Christ's command. 2. Prove or justify that the command makes rational sense before obeying. 3. Trust Christ's wisdom and accept that even His foolishness was greater than human wisdom. The disciples chose the third option.

The middle road—the "third way"—is better than falling off the path on either side, or turning to the right hand or to the left. Neither Job's wife, who cursed God as the cause of her husband's troubles, nor Job's friends, who tried to defend the Lord, were right. As the philosopher Hegel might say, taking the best from a thesis and its antithesis provides a synthesis.[24] Conservatives are too often afraid of questions, and liberals may fear answers, but hopefully we do not need to be terrified of either.[25]

In dealing with the issues of origins we must have Christians who are both dedicated to Scripture and intellectually responsible. Many of one type or the other are available, but few have both qualities. Too many intellectually responsible academics give up on the church. Other Christians are zealous for God, but unenlightened.

How should church employees—professors, pastors, and evangelists—as well as ordinary members present the topic of origins? A few offer only standard evolution theories, while others advocate indefensible creation speculations. Both lead hearers astray. Perhaps a humble, unifying attitude is more important for everyone than a preference for a specific scientific model.

Relationships

I've wondered for many years what my church has to offer those with an academic, particularly a scientific, mind-set. This mind-set is widespread in secular society since science and technology affect every area of life. The church can carefully define its doctrinal position about origins, but theological pronouncements do not solve scientific issues, so doctrinal affirmations do little to meet the needs of the cultural scientific mind-set. Academics are interested in an intellectually coherent worldview—one that fits with their firsthand intellectual experience.

Seventh-day Adventists are well positioned to address such needs. We have a history of respect for and emphasis on education[26] and are intellectually responsible and academically respectable. This has been especially true in the area of science, both because we see the world as God's creation and because of our medical emphasis. The General Conference Education Department, through its Faith and Learning seminars, has stressed integrating Christian belief with academic excellence.

During my years as a student and later a postdoctoral researcher in secular universities, fellow students and professors would often ask about my church. The following types of responses are based on a number of such experiences.

Argument. We are to decide "from weight of evidence,"[27] and some of the best evidence for a Creator is that of inherent design. Several scientists have independently brought up this evidence in my discussions with them. Note, however, that such design arguments are not part of the scientific method or a political agenda.

The movie *12 Angry Men*★ graphically demonstrates how different arguments convince different people. A jury begins deliberations with an almost unanimous guilty vote against a young minority man accused of murder. The one dissenting voter feels that a death sentence conviction needs to be carefully thought through. In the ensuing discussion, one juror alters his vote as he recognizes a reasonable doubt. Others change their minds based on additional evidence or after reasoning through the alibi. One vacillating man shifts his vote several times and another reverses his vote just to speed up the proceedings. Two jurors have background issues—one is a racist bigot and the other is estranged from his son—and reverse their votes only after being forced to realize their own underlying prejudices.

All arguments used in the issue of origins must be sound. Augustine noted that the gospel loses credibility when we present interpretations that unbelievers know are incorrect. Ad hoc answers to origins questions are like the fig tree with leaves but no fruit (Mark 11:13, 14).

Argumentation has its place, but it seems to be limited. In arguments with my wife, I may have impeccable logic, but she still wins. The Christian defender of the faith faces the danger of seeing the doctrines as no stronger than his weak arguments.[28] Paul made an eloquent presentation to the Athenians on Mars Hill (Acts 17:16-34), but then determined to present only Christ in Corinth (1 Cor. 2:2-4).[29]

Humility. Christians would do well to remember that "we know in part" (1 Cor. 13:9). Madeleine L'Engle appreciates scientists who are willing to say "This is how it appears now" over theologians who believe they have the final answers.[30]

As individuals we need to keep in mind our own weaknesses. When someone asked G. K. Chesterton what was wrong with the world, he responded, "I am."[31] Solzhenitsyn recognized that the "line between good and evil runs through the heart of every individual."[32] And Oswald Chambers observed, "It takes God a long time to get us to stop thinking that unless everyone sees things exactly as we do, they must be wrong."[33]

"We draw people to Christ not by loudly discrediting what they believe, by telling them how wrong they are and how right we are, but by showing them a light that is so lovely that they want with all their hearts to know the source of it."[34] Elsewhere L'Engle observes that *The Secret Garden* "is more successful than *Little Lord Fauntleroy*, for instance, because it is a better piece of storytelling, less snobbish, and the message doesn't show, like a slip hanging below the hem of a dress."[35]

Honesty and Integrity With Evidence. No one will listen to us until we have earned their trust and respect. To lose the respect of others because we are people of faith is nothing to be ashamed of, but to lose respect because of our snide remarks, haughtiness, dogmatism, evolution bashing, or poorly informed comments is inexcusable.

Truth can afford to be fair and look at all the data, for this is how God presents Himself in Scripture. Some have compared creationists to tobacco company scientists who get paid to find only supportive evidence, so in my own work I go out of my way to include the data I discover that doesn't seem to fit my paradigm. Presenting both sides decreases the risk of a later crisis of faith, when listeners might find out "the rest of the story." Half-truths make apologetics easier in the short run, but God doesn't need to win by stacking the deck.

Honesty rejects the use of sensational claims and scientific overstatement. Well-meaning Christians have so often made such claims that we need to go out of our way to remedy the situation. The most useful worldview is a natural outgrowth of the full range of data, not a forced or contrived organization of some of the facts.

Overstating the words of inspiration is also counterproductive.[36] For example, the Adventist Church doesn't believe in the verbal inspiration of the Bible or extreme literalism when interpreting obviously metaphorical or other stylistic devices. The unfounded belief of 200 years ago that the Bible teaches fixity of species resulted in a swing to the opposite direction after Darwin.

Friendship. Building bridges instead of walls should be obvious, but our attitudes toward scientists too often antagonize and alienate. Scientists are not enemies, but fellow travelers in a search for truth.

Winning people is more important than winning arguments. Winning arguments wins neither, while winning people leads to both. In dealing with Thomas's doubts, Jesus didn't reproach His disciple or enter into controversy, but simply revealed Himself (John 20:24-28).[37]

My wife manages a diabetes treatment center and often interacts with pharmaceutical representatives. At a luncheon one of these reps unexpectedly said that he and his family were interested in the Seventh-day Adventist Church, because he had enjoyed working with Adventist medical personnel. Startled, Debbie responded, "You want to do what?" During the next few months they started attending church, studied with one of the pastors, and were baptized. To complete the story, we visited them as they moved into their new house and noticed that the house next door was for sale. We are now neighbors.

The wife had grown up in Hungary, attended Communist schools, trained in chemistry, and worked on a doctoral program in psychology. Because of her early education in Communism, she asked a little about creationism. I made a few comments, and she heard some discussions on design, but it really was a minor issue, because her mind-set was ready for a change. Excellent arguments without friendship have little effect, whereas friendship with few arguments can make a difference.

Conclusion

How then do I deal with uncertainty, paradox, and conflict? Inspired sources do not always give me the best scientific explanation of the natural world; however, I am willing to recognize that God's foolishness is greater than my wisdom (1 Cor. 1:25) and to believe in spite of uncertainty. The book of Job confirms that approach: His wife saw the problems and refused to believe. Job's friends believed and refused to see the problems. Job, however, believed while still recognizing the problems, as represented by his statement "Though he slay me, yet will I trust in him: but I will maintain [margin: prove, or argue] mine own ways before him" (Job 13:15, KJV).

I am sympathetic to church members who would like definitive answers about the question of origins and of church leaders who want unity on the issue. In return, I hope for understanding of the difficult position in which I and other scientists find ourselves. We must intentionally nurture the church's best and brightest intellects who are devoted to Jesus Christ as Lord, but are unwilling to accept superficial scientific answers. As a scientist, I may appear to bow to the "god of science" as Naaman bowed with his master in a Syrian temple, but as Naaman told Elisha: "Your servant will not offer burnt offering or sacrifice to any god but the Lord" (2 Kings 5:17, RSV).

I have taken the story of the Gadarene demoniacs as my example. Even though they could not answer doctrinal questions, they could tell what Jesus had done in their life (Mark 5:19).[38] Although I don't have nearly as many answers about origins as I would like, I do trust Jesus as the central figure in every issue discussed in these chapters.

A Theological Perspective of the Tower of Babel

After their creation God told Adam and Eve that He wanted them to populate the world with human beings (Gen. 1:28). He repeated His desire to Noah and his family after the Flood, asking them to spread across the entire world (Gen. 9:1). But the human race refused to do so out of a fear that God would scatter them against their will (Gen. 11:4), perhaps remembering what had happened to Cain. They considered His plan for them as actually a threat to their survival. Rejecting the divine command, they decided to build a city and then a tower where they could remain together. In addition, they wanted to "make a name" for themselves.

Previously in the book of Genesis the pattern has always been that of a superior giving a name to someone: God to His creation (Gen. 1:5, 8, 10); Adam to the animals (Gen. 2:20); a husband to his wife (because of the curse of male dominion placed on Eve [Gen. 3:20]); and parents to children (Gen. 4:25, 26; 5:3). But the people of Shinar violated the pattern by seeking to establish a name through their own initiative.

In an act of rebellion against God's intent for the human race they constructed the city and tower from fired brick mortared together with bitumen, or asphalt. The alluvial plains of the Euphrates and Tigris rivers lack sources of building stone. People had to import it from distant mountains at great effort and expense. Most Mesopotamian buildings consisted of mud or clay brick. But the terse literary style of Scripture, which rarely goes into detail or description, probably mentions the use of the bricks and asphalt mortar for a reason of its own. When the people of Shinar built something in opposition to God, they used extremely flimsy materials. The tower could not go very high before it would begin crumbling under its weight. But the Lord did not wait until the project collapsed by itself. He blocked their efforts by transforming their single human language into several. The people who wanted to make a name for themselves still did exactly that. Their city, which they called "gate of the gods," became Babel, which biblical tradition, employing a similar-sounding Hebrew word, consistently translates as "confusion" (Gen. 11:9).

★ See p. 17.

[1] E. G. White, *Patriarchs and Prophets,* p. 119.

[2] Bryan Magee, *The Story of Philosophy* (London: Dorling Kindersley, 2001), pp. 205, 206.

[3] F. David Peat, *From Certainty to Uncertainty: The Story of Science and Idea in the Twentieth Century* (Washington, D.C.: Joseph Henry Press, 2002), pp. 73, 74, 86.

[4] D. Atkinson, *The Message of Genesis 1-11,* pp. 189, 190.

[5] S. Weinberg, *Dreams of a Final Theory,* pp. 247, 248.

[6] C. S. Lewis, *Miracles* (New York: Macmillan, 1960).

[7] M. A. Noll, *The Scandal of the Evangelical Mind,* pp. 85-104.

[8] In M. L'Engle, *Walking on Water,* p. 28.

[9] Noll, p. 125.

[10] Peat.

[11] G. S. Stent, *Paradoxes of Free Will,* p. 1.

[12] *Ibid.,* pp. 7, 9.

[13] E. G. White, *The Desire of Ages,* pp. 87, 88.

[14] *Ibid.,* p. 762.

[15] *Ibid.,* pp. 603-606.

[16] P. Yancey, *Disappointment With God,* pp. 234, 235.

[17] White, *The Desire of Ages,* p. 414.

[18] In Atkinson, p. 66.

[19] Ellen G. White, *Steps to Christ* (Chicago: Fleming H. Revell, 1892), p. 105.

[20] In Tom Morris, *Philosophy for Dummies* (New York: Wiley, 1999), p. 332.

[21] Allan Sandage, interview by Philip Clayton and "Science and Religion: Separate Closets in the Same House," in W. Mark Richardson et al., eds., *Science and the Spiritual Quest: New Essays by Leading Scientists* (New York: Routledge, 2002), pp. 52-63.

[22] Ellen G. White, *The Ministry of Healing* (Mountain View, Calif.: Pacific Press Pub. Assn., 1905), pp. 411, 412; *Education,* p. 99.

[23] White, *Patriarchs and Prophets,* p. 115.

[24] Magee, p. 159.

[25] P. Kreeft, *Making Sense Out of Suffering,* p. 183.

[26] White, *The Desire of Ages,* p. 249; *Education.*

[27] White, *The Desire of Ages,* p. 458.

[28] C. S. Lewis, *God in the Dock: Essays on Theology and Ethics* (Grand Rapids: Eerdmans, 1970), p. 103; see also White, *Testimonies,* vol. 5, pp. 705, 706.

[29] Ellen G. White, *The Acts of the Apostles* (Mountain View, Calif.: Pacific Press Pub. Assn., 1911), pp. 235-254.

[30] M. L'Engle, *Walking on Water,* p. 231.

[31] In Yancey, *Soul Survivor,* p. 58.

[32] Aleksandr I. Solzhenitsyn, *The Gulag Archipelago: 1918-1956* (New York: Harper and Row, 1974), vol. 1, p. 168.

[33] Oswald Chambers, *My Utmost for His Highest* (Grand Rapids: Discovery House Pubs., 1992), May 6.

[34] L'Engle, pp. 140, 141; see also White, *The Desire of Ages,* p. 299.

[35] L'Engle, p. 143.

[36] White, *The Desire of Ages,* p. 29.

[37] *Ibid.,* p. 808.

[38] *Ibid.,* p. 340.

7

Blessing a Broken World
Genesis 11:27-15:21[1]

At first glance Genesis 1-11 (often described as the primeval history) may seem to have been tacked on to the rest of the book (the ancestral history of God's people) and to have little connection with what comes afterward. But the two sections are two sides of a single coin. The Lord commences the first 11 chapters by creating. The rest of the book He spends redeeming. "God's act of creation began with God speaking: 'And God said, "Let there be light"'" (Gen. 1:3, NIV). His act of redemption also begins with God speaking: 'The Lord had said to Abram, "Leave your country . . ."'" (Gen. 12:1, NIV). Each of the two major parts of Genesis begins with a speech from God, because without him neither creation nor redemption can happen. God spoke his initial words of creation in the middle of physical chaos. He now speaks his words of redemption in the shadow of Babel's moral chaos."[2]

But the two sections of Genesis are linked in additional ways. Genesis 11 speaks of a two-part human migration (first to the plain of Shinar, then across the face of the earth [verse 2]) and a desire to "make a name" (verse 4). Then Genesis 12 has God calling for Abram to migrate in two stages to another land (first to Haran and finally to Canaan [Gen. 11:31; 12:1]) with the promise that his name will be made great (Gen. 12:2). The biblical author thus intricately binds together the primeval and ancestral histories.

The Line of Shem
After surveying all of humanity, Genesis now focuses on one single

83

family line—the descendants of Shem (a name meaning, literally, "name"), culminating in Terah (Gen. 11:10-32). Like the rest of the human race, this line also migrates, but instead of going east, it travels westward to Ur of the Chaldees.

For a long time the only city named Ur that scholars knew about was the Sumerian one on the southern Euphrates River. It puzzled them why Genesis 11:28 called it Ur of the Chaldees since that people lived in northern Mesopotamia. Then archaeologists found ancient Mesopotamian texts that referred to a smaller town named Ur in the north not far from Haran, the city where Terah settled his family for a time.[3] Elsewhere Genesis lists Abraham's family as coming from Paddan-aram (Gen. 28:2) or Aram Naharaim (Gen. 24:10), areas also located in the region of northern Mesopotamia located between the Tigris and Euphrates rivers.

The genealogies of Genesis 5 and 10 emphasize the continuity of life. Genesis 5 ended with the birth of Noah's sons. Genesis 10 has humanity spreading across the earth. But the genealogy of Genesis 11 concludes with death. Terah dies, and his son marries a barren woman. The family line seemed doomed to extinction. The ancients would have considered this fate an infinite tragedy.

Barrenness was always something that frightened the people of the ancient world. While modern humanity worries about overpopulation, the ancients realized that the human race was always one generation from extinction. Disease, drought, crop failure, accidents, and war made life precarious. Unlike the situation in the modern Western world, in which children are an economic liability, children in the ancient world became economic assets as soon as age 5 or 6. Families needed as many children as possible to work the farm and in home crafts. In the home itself they could gather firewood and other fuel, and help in cooking.[4]

The ancients considered children a blessing from God. The more one had, clearly the more He had blessed. On the other hand, childlessness represented a curse from the Lord that had great impact on life. Sons and daughters would take care of their parents as they aged and became more feeble and then give them a proper burial when they died. And the head of every household wanted sons to pass on to and preserve the family estate. It was a concern that worried even the upper classes. Two epic ballads from the ancient Syrian city of Ugarit tell of Keret and Dan'il, royal figures who struggled to obtain heirs.

The Call of Abram

Abram first appears in the biblical record not as a young man but at age 75. Scripture says that he lived to the age of 175. The biblical record covers only the last 100 years of his life and particularly dwells on his hundredth year. Genesis 12 through 24 consists of 19 literary units.[5] Five chapters forming eight literary units dwell on that special year, showing its importance to the biblical writer.

Scripture never really explains the mechanisms of how God communicates to humanity. It just declares that He speaks, and the ones that He reveals Himself to accept that His message is divine. To Abram He said, "Go from your country and your kindred and your father's house to the land that I will show you" (Gen. 12:1).

Joshua 24:2 and 14 indicate that Abram came from a family of polytheists. He must have had some knowledge of the Lord, but how much we do not know. Walton and Matthews suggest that his family shared the general religious concepts of the time. The kind of gods they visualized "did not reveal their natures or give any idea of what would bring their favor or wrath. They were worshiped by being flattered, cajoled, humored and appeased. *Manipulation* is the operative term."[6] But the God of Scripture wanted to change that understanding. And He did it in a surprising way— through a covenant. "When he appears to Abraham, he does not give him a doctrinal statement or require rituals or issue demands; he makes an offer. . . . He says that he has something to give Abraham if Abraham is willing to give up some things first."[7]

People in the ancient world could survive only within the confines of the extended family. It was almost impossible for single individuals (or even what we today call nuclear families) to survive by themselves. When Abram left Haran, he gave up his right to inherit the family estate, especially land, the ultimate source of all wealth. "Land, family and inheritance were among the most significant elements in ancient society. For farmers and herdsmen land was their livelihood. For city dwellers land represented their political identity. Descendants represented the future."[8] Thus Abram forfeited his economic security and put himself, Sarai, and his retainers at great risk. God asked him to abandon what he had and to trust Him to give him something greater.

To Bless the Nations

But Abram would not be the only recipient of the divine promise. Through him God would bless all the families of the earth (Gen. 12:2, 3).

They would be the people the Lord had scattered from Babel (Gen. 11:9). "When God calls Abram he doesn't simply call him to enjoy a special relationship with him. He calls him to be a part of God's scheme for history, in which the tragedy we have seen in the primeval history will finally be overturned, and the world redeemed from the curse of sin. From the chaos of sin God's new order will emerge through the one who came as the descendant of Abraham and the Word of God. 'Since we have been justified through faith, we have peace with God through our Lord Jesus Christ' (Romans 5:1, NIV)."[9] The book of Genesis as a whole tells of God's blessing given to His creation, God's blessing lost, and God's blessing restored.

The divine summons to leave would affect not only Abram. With him went his servants and retainers. God's call to the patriarch uprooted them also. They left Haran where Terah had settled and followed the Fertile Crescent to Canaan, the region along the Mediterranean coast wedged between the ancient civilizations of Mesopotamia and Egypt. Abram, his people, and his vast flocks wandered through the land until they came to the ancient city of Shechem.

Archaeologists place Shechem at Tell Balatah, east of modern Nablus and 35 miles north of Jerusalem. Located at the east entrance to the pass between Mount Gerizim and Mount Ebal, it was a major trading center. There God appeared to Abram and announced, "To your offspring I will give this land" (Gen. 12:7). The patriarch constructed an altar that introduced worship of the true God in the Promised Land. Shechem would become a religious center to God's people. From Shechem Abram journeyed to Bethel and erected still another altar. All his altars symbolized the future occupation of the Promised Land. Many of the sites would later become major Israelite religious centers.

Taking Refuge in Egypt

As we have observed before, life was precarious in the ancient world. Famine was just one of the greater dangers facing it. Farmers and herders in Palestine had to depend upon the sometimes-unreliable rainfall. But the constant flow of the Nile in Egypt and the fact that the people could irrigate their fields made life more secure there. As the famine worsened in Canaan, Abram decided to relocate his extensive household there until the emergency passed. But he saw a potential danger as he entered Egypt, and it involved his wife.

"I know well that you are a woman beautiful in appearance," he told her. "And when the Egyptians see you, they will say, 'This is his wife';

86

then they will kill me, but they will let you live. Say you are my sister" (verses 11-13). Interestingly, ancient Egyptian love poetry referred to one's beloved as "sister" or "brother."[10] Also of interest is the fact that the biblical world considered sibling relationships closer than marriage ties.[11] Marriage provided heirs, but people looked to their brothers and sisters for emotional support and loyalty. In a perhaps unconscious way Abram might have been actually complimenting his relationship with Sarai.

But it still cannot be denied that Abram passed off his wife as his sister to save his own skin. The theme of wife as sister appears three times in the book of Genesis. "All three wife-sister stories in Genesis (chaps. 12, 20, 26) have in common that the foreign monarch is more concerned about morality than is the patriarch."[12] The motivation behind the ruse was possibly that while a ruler might negotiate with a brother to gain a woman as wife, he might just eliminate a husband and avoid the expense and bargaining involved in arranging a marital contract. Another interpretation has Abram hoping "that by claiming to be Sarai's brother he could fend off suitors by promises of marriage without actually giving her away. This suggestion is confirmed by other stories where brothers try to delay their sisters' marriages (Gen. 24:55, Laban and Rebekah; Gen. 34:13-17, Dinah and her brothers)."[13] But whatever the reason for the subterfuge, it shows a lack of faith in God's power to protect Abram and later Isaac.

While the phrase the Egyptian officials used to describe Sarai (Gen. 12:14, 15) can apply to a woman's physical attractiveness (2 Sam. 14:27), it can also refer to a man's good looks (1 Sam. 17:42) and even to the appearance of a cow (Gen. 41:2). "We need not therefore assume that Sarah has miraculously retained the stunning beauty of youth. Her dignity, her bearing, her countenance, her outfitting could all contribute to the impression that she is a striking woman."[14] Most likely Pharaoh would have wanted marriage to Sarai as a way of forming a political alliance with an obviously wealthy and influential tribal leader. Egyptian rulers frequently established political ties through marriage. Abram headed a significant tribal group from Canaan, an area that Egypt had long regarded as its sphere of influence. Gaining Sarah as a wife would thus establish a marital (and political) alliance with Abram.

The king knew nothing about Abram's duplicity, but God sent plagues (perhaps some sort of skin disease) upon the royal household to warn Pharaoh that something was wrong. It is the kind of divine communication the ancients took seriously. When the king discovered Abram's deception, he immediately summoned the patriarch. "What is this you have done to me?" he demanded (Gen. 12:18). "The royal anger is conveyed in the rapid succession of accusatory questions and the brusque expulsion order. Abram offers no justification of his conduct. He and his wife are quickly escorted out of Egypt."[15] But, as we shall see, Abram seems to learn nothing from the experience. In fact, it has only made him wealthier (verses 16, 20).

Besides letting us know Abram's need for spiritual growth, the story also sets a literary pattern for the eventual Exodus narrative. Israel goes into Egypt because of famine, a plague strikes, and God's people get expelled (the word used in Genesis 13 appears when Pharaoh sends the Hebrew slaves away) after receiving gifts from the Egyptians. But the Egyptian king here is quite different than the pharaoh of the Exodus. He displays more ethical sense than Abraham does.

Lot and Abram Part Ways

Abram's flocks were even larger after he left Egypt. As a resident alien, he would have to negotiate with the people of Canaan to graze his animals on their land and to use their water supplies. Suitable pastureland and springs or wells were limited in Palestine, and the local inhabitants would have had first rights to everything. Whatever they permitted him to use, Abram would have had to share it with Lot. Their shepherds began quarreling with each other about how to parcel out the limited resources. (Although the biblical text does not mention it, Lot and Abram's servants would also have had run-ins with the local people simply because of the sheer size of the combined herds.)

Abram attempted to work out a solution to the problem that would end the disputes (Gen. 13:8, 9). The casual reader might assume that they were dividing the land between them. But they did not own any of it. What Abram sought to do was to find a way, in a manner that would reduce conflict, that they could use what land and water rights the people of the region granted them.

Shepherds grazed their flocks on the lower elevations during the rainy months of October through March, then shifted them to higher elevations during the hot dry season of April through September. Grass would continue to grow and springs to flow in the highlands. The herds migrated in a regular cycle. Lot and Abram had to shift their flocks in a way so they would not be in the same place at the same time. Abram suggested that they work out an itinerary that would prevent their flocks from exhausting the grass and water at any one spot. The older man gave the younger first choice. Proper protocol would have required that the nephew defer to his uncle. But the younger man made his selection first. He decided to move his flocks and household to the plain of the Jordan (verses 10, 11).

Most readers assume that Lot greedily chose the best part of the land, but what he did was even worse than that. The cities of the plain were outside of the traditional biblical boundaries of the Promised Land (see especially Numbers 34:1–12). By going there, he was rejecting the divine promise God had made to his uncle.[16] Ironically, while much of the region along the Jordan appears green and luxuriant from a distance, it is really a tangled and inhospitable maze. In ancient times the depression through which the river flows (the zor, or "thicket"), with its junglelike vegetation, was the haunt of many wild animals. Furthermore, the text says that Lot went east (Gen. 13:11). In Genesis the direction of east has sinister connotations, perhaps indicating something outside of God's special domain (cf. Gen. 4:16). Lot settled near Sodom. The biblical writer, who rarely intruded himself into the story, now specifically mentioned that "the people of Sodom were wicked, great sinners against the Lord" (Gen. 13:13). The fact that the narrator commented at all showed how seriously he viewed their lifestyle.

Abram, however, remained in Canaan (verse 12). Lot had "looked" around and chosen Sodom (verse 10). After the nephew left, God told Abram, *"Look* from the place where you are . . . ; for all the land that you see I will give to you and to your offspring forever" (verses 14, 15). The patriarch, who had neither land nor offspring, would receive both if he continued to trust in the God who had led him to Canaan. So far he had not abandoned the land—and the divine promise—as his nephew Lot had. The aged man with the barren wife would have descendants "like the dust of the earth" (verse 16). And God would give him the whole land, not just a part of it.

Lot settled in a region that he thought would be "like the garden of the Lord" (verse 10)—a veritable Eden. But not only was it a wicked place—even more evil entered it. A coalition of four marauding kings invaded it just as the serpent did the original Paradise.

The kings were out for plunder, not conquest. They marched south along the major trade artery often referred to as the King's Highway. It ran north-south just east of the Jordan Valley. Five local rulers attempted to repulse them in the Valley of Siddim, but found themselves overwhelmed. Fleeing, the kings of Sodom and Gomorrah[17] hid in a cluster of bitumen pits. The others fled to the nearby hills. After sacking Sodom and

Gomorrah and capturing Lot and his family (possibly for ransom), the raiders went west and up that side of the Jordan.

One man who managed to escape told Abram what had happened (Gen. 14:13). The narrative refers to Abram as "the Hebrew." Many scholars see it not as an ethnic term, but a social designation indicating that he was landless and thus holding only a marginal position in Canaanite society.[18]

Abram assembled his men to pursue the invaders. Egyptian and other ancient documents indicate that ancient armies were usually quite small in number. Abram's private force of 318 would have been equivalent to that fielded by many major powers. Apparently some others joined Abram's band (verse 24). Catching up with the kings near what would be the city of Dan, he attacked them at night. Nighttime ambush was a common military tactic. Egyptian and Hittite documents refer to it. He divided his forces, probably to strike from more than one direction. The patriarch routed the raiders and followed them beyond Damascus. Then he returned Lot, the other captives, and the booty to the Dead Sea area.

Once he arrived back south, Abram had two visitors: the king of Sodom and Melchizedek, the priest-king of Salem.[19] It was quite common in the ancient world for a ruler to be both king and priest. Melchizedek was priest of God Most High, whom Scripture identifies with Yahweh, God of Israel (cf. Ps. 47:2; 57:2; 78:35, 56). The priest-king brought wine and bread, symbolizing a royal banquet, to the triumphant Abram, and then blessed the patriarch (verses 19, 20). God had said that Abram would bless the nations. The patriarch's successful rescue of the captives was the first tangible fulfillment of the divine promise.[20] Melchizedek declared that the "maker of heaven and earth" had blessed Abram, a phrase that directs the reader of Genesis back to the beginning of the book as well as advancing the theme of Creation that will weave itself throughout the rest of Scripture. In response, Abram gave the king a tenth, or tithe, of the booty.[21] Abram would have divided the plunder recaptured from the raiders into 10 piles and given one of them to Melchizedek.

The king of Sodom asked only for the captives back, stating that Abram could keep the booty (verse 21). Abram refused to hold on to any of it lest the king might claim that he had made the patriarch rich (verses 22, 23). The only thing that he would retain was the food supplies for his men and enough plunder to pay the allies who had accompanied him on the expedition.

The story contrasts Melchizedek and the king of Sodom. Melchizedek had brought bread and wine and blessed the patriarch. Ancient society showered successful military leaders with gifts. But the king of Sodom offered nothing to the man who had risked his life and the lives of his people to save the captives abducted from the cities of the plain. Instead, the king asked for something, making "a short, almost rude demand of just six words: 'Give me people; take property yourself.' There is none of the customary courtesy here. The word order (note how he mentions 'giving' before 'taking') reflects Sodom's ungracious self-centeredness."[22] The narrator has begun to demonstrate the truthfulness of God's later verdict on the people of the plain (Gen. 18:16-19:29).

Covenant With Abram

Sometime after Abram's dramatic rescue of Lot, "the word of the Lord came to Abram in a vision" (Gen. 15:1), the common phrase introducing a divine message to a prophet in the Old Testament. "Do not be afraid," God told him. "I am your shield; your reward shall be very great." Using a military image, God promised protection for him in his precarious status in Canaan. But that security seemed worthless to Abram. What good was it when he still had no children—no heir? "O Lord God, what will you give me, for I continue childless, and the heir of my house is Eliezer of Damascus?" (verse 2). Sometimes this need for children to preserve the family line, inherit the family property, and care for aging parents would be met through adoption.[23] Abram suggested the adoption solution to God (verse 3).

The Lord immediately rejected the idea. Abram's heir would be not adopted, "but your very own issue" (verse 4). Taking him outside, the Lord instructed him to look up at the night sky and try to count the stars. Alluding to their great number, He declared, "So shall your descendants be" (verse 5). The narrator now interrupted the story to make a vital point: "And he believed the Lord; and the Lord reckoned it to him as righteousness" (verse 6).

"There appear to be two reasons why Abram's faith should be noted here: (1) because the word of promise had come to him in a crisis situation following the battle of chapter 14, and (2) it serves as a reminder of Abram's attitude to God, which should be a model for all his descendants to follow."[24]

Because Abram believed God's promise, the Lord regarded that trust in Him as "righteousness." Allusions to righteousness appear several times in the book of Genesis. It is not an abstract inner quality that people have or achieve on their own. Generally "righteousness might well be paraphrased as God-like, or at least God-pleasing, action. This sense of Godapproved behavior is apparent in Genesis 18:19; 30:33; 38:26."[25] But Abram has done nothing except to take God at His word. "Normally righteousness results in acquittal by the divine judge. Here faith, the right response to God's revelation, counts instead. As the rest of the story makes plain, this faith leads to righteous action (e.g., Gen. 18:19), but only here in the Old Testament is it counted as righteousness."[26]

Abram's faith centered in something specific—God and His promises. The New Testament would later use the story to demonstrate that justification has always been by faith, or trust, in God (Rom. 4:3; Gal. 3:6; James 2:23) and that true faith manifests itself through concrete action (James 2:18).

God's original promise to Abram (Gen. 12:1-3) involved not only descendants but a land for them to live in that was their own. The Lord has just reaffirmed that the patriarch will have physical offspring. Now he turns to the issue of their territory. "I am the Lord who brought you from Ur of the Chaldeans, to give you this land to possess" (Gen. 15:7). Abram has now spent many years as a sojourner—a resident alien—in Canaan and is extremely aware that not a square inch of it really belongs to him. "O Lord God, how am I to know that I shall possess it?" (verse 8).

Although Abram has faith, it needs to grow. The Lord uses the power of enacted ritual to expand that faith. He has the patriarch bring a heifer, a female goat, and a ram—all 3 years old—as well as a turtledove and a young pigeon. They are the types and ages of animals used in sacrifices. Except for the birds, He has Abram cut them in two (verses 9, 10). God is guaranteeing His promise of the land by making a covenant with Abram. The Hebrew term used to refer to the making of a covenant literally means "to cut" a covenant. Ancient nonbiblical texts also mention the slaughter of animals as part of the process of treatymaking.

For a while Abram fights off the ever-present birds of prey (verse 11), then, as the sun sets, he falls into a deep sleep (verse 12). The "deep sleep" and the "terrifying darkness" echo biblical images of divine activity and the awe that it triggers (cf. Gen. 2:21; Ex. 10:21, 22; 14:20; 15:16; 23:27; Deut. 4:11; Joshua 2:9; Isa. 29:10). Such phenomena would also occur during the Exodus from Egypt and Israel's conquest of the Promised Land, events that God now prophesies about (Gen. 15:13-16). Abram's descendants, God reveals, will be slaves for 400 years, but they will eventually go free and leave with great possessions (echoing Genesis 12:16). They will return to Canaan. Lest the prophecy discourage Abram, God assures him that he will live to a good old age (Gen. 15:15), the ideal life from the perspective of the ancients.

After the sun had set, Abram saw a smoking firepot and a flaming torch pass between the severed bodies of the animals. The familiar objects were a theophany, a manifestation of God's presence. The Lord would repeat the theophany on a grander scale by the pillar of cloud and fire in the book of Exodus. God next formally announced the covenant with the patriarch, declaring, "To your descendants I give this land, from the river of Egypt to the great river, the river Euphrates" (verse 18).

What God does for Abram parallels what the ancients knew as a "royal grant" covenant. A king used it to reward the loyalty of a servant or a vassal. Instead of its obligations falling on the inferior party, the king would impose them upon himself. Grants involving land would of course have its boundaries defined. God does this in verse 18. The king of the universe has covenanted to give the land of Canaan to Abram.

---

[1] The biblical author divides Genesis into a prologue (Genesis 1:1-2:3) and 10 episodes through the use of the Hebrew phrase *'elleh toledot* ("these are the generations of"). See Genesis 2:4; 5:1; 6:9; 10:1; 11:10; 11:27; 25:12; 25:19; 36:1; 36:9 (repeated for Esau); 37:2. The structure ties the book together as a whole. The patriarchal narratives thus actually start in Genesis 11:27 instead of Genesis 12:1.

[2] Turner, *Back to the Present,* p. 106; cf. Tremper Longman III, *How to Read Genesis* (Downers Grove, Ill.: InterVarsity Press, 2005), p. 64.

[3] John H. Walton and Victor H. Matthews, *The IVP Bible Background Commentary: Genesis-Deuteronomy* (Downers Grove, Ill: InterVarsity Press, 1997), p. 35.

[4] For a discussion of the economic role of children, see Carol Meyers, "The Family in Early Israel," in Leo G. Perdue et. al., *Families in Ancient Israel* (Louisville: Westminster John Knox Press, 1997), pp. 25-32.

[5] Jan Fokkelman, *Reading Biblical Narrative: An Introductory Guide,* trans. Ineke Smit (Louisville: Westminster John Knox Press, 1999), p. 212.

[6] Walton and Matthews, p. 36.

[7] *Ibid.*

[8] *Ibid.,* p. 35.

[9] Turner, p. 108.

[10] Miriam Lichtheim, *ancient Egyptian Literature* (Berkeley, Calif.: University of California Press, 1976), Vol. II, p. 181.

[11] Joseph H. Hellerman, *The Ancient Church as Family* (Minneapolis: Fortress Press, 2001), pp. 36-39. Although Hellerman focuses on the early church as a surrogate kinship group, he first shows how families functioned in both the Old and New Testament worlds before demonstrating how Christianity sought to duplicate that social structure within the church itself. See especially the chapter "Mediterranean Family Systems" (pp. 27-58) for background on ancient family organization.

[12] G. J. Wenham, *Genesis 1-15,* p. 291.

[13] *Ibid.*, p. 288.

[14] Walton and Matthews, p. 37.

[15] Wenham, p. 289.

[16] Wenham has Lot, at best, only on the very edge of Canaan (*ibid.*, pp. 297, 299).

[17] The names of the two kings are compound ones that include the words "evil" and "wicked." "Deliberate Hebrew mispronunciation of these kings' names from early times with a view to emphasizing their sinfulness seems quite likely" (*ibid.*, p. 309). The allusion to evil foreshadows the ultimate destruction of them and their people.

[18] Scholars debate whether the word is somehow related to 'Apiru, a term found in the Egyptian Armana tablets and other ancient documents (see *Eerdmans Dictionary of the Bible*, ed. David Noel Freedman [Grand Rapids: Eerdmans, 2000], p. 567). Many see the word as referring to social class (landless individuals) rather than to ethnicity.

[19] Although tradition and most scholars equate Salem with the later city of Jerusalem, the sixth-century Madaba map associates it with the city of Shechem.

[20] Wenham, p. 317. Wenham suggests that by blessing Abram, Melchizedek would himself be blessed.

[21] Ten percent was the typical tax percentage levied by Late Bronze Age states (George E. Mendenhall, *Ancient Israel's Faith and History: An Introduction to the Bible in Context* [Louisville: Westminster John Knox Press, 2001], p. 107. In ancient Egypt either the king (who was considered a god on earth) or the various temples owned most of the land. Those who farmed such lands had to pay a 10 percent rent on them.

[22] Wenham, p. 318.

[23] Victor H. Matthews, "Marriage and Family in the Ancient Near East," in *Marriage and Family in the Biblical Word,* ed. Ken M. Campbell (Downers Grove, Ill.: InterVarsity Press, 2003), pp. 18-20.

[24] Wenham, p. 329.

[25] *Ibid.*, p. 330. We will look at certain aspects of righteousness in the story of Tamar (Gen. 38).

[26] *Ibid.*

8

Searching for a Son
Genesis 16-19

Motherhood formed a major part of a woman's self-identity in the ancient world. Sarai lived in a culture that narrowly defined the role and status of women by their relationship to men, specifically husbands and sons. Although she was a wife, Sarai was not a mother, let alone the mother of a son. From the perspective of patriarchal culture she was not even a full-fledged member of Abraham's family. The ancients (as well as modern patriarchal cultures) defined a family relative as one who had a blood relationship with the male head of a family. A wife would be considered a part of the family once she bore sons.[1]

Because her identity was less than it should have been, it may have been a further motivation for Sarai to become a surrogate mother through Hagar. In addition, a childless woman considered herself incomplete and even punished by God. A number of ancient cultures accepted the custom of substitute childbearing, and Sarai seized on such a concept to deal with her childlessness.[2] Ancient society regarded slave women as legal extensions of their female owners. As one of her household duties Hagar could conceive children for Sarai.[3] She pressured her husband, "'You see that the Lord has prevented me from bearing children; go in to my slave-girl; it may be that I shall obtain children by her.' And Abram listened to the voice of Sarai" (Gen. 16:2). Instead of the voice of God, Abraham listened to that of his wife.[4]

But when Ishmael was born, Sarai discovered that she was still not happy—that she still craved her own child. To add to her misery, Hagar "looked with contempt on her mistress" (verse 4), perhaps from the feeling that she was a real woman since she could have a child and Sarai couldn't. Sarai then focused her hurt and disappointment on her husband. "May the Lord judge between you and me!" (verse 5). But he had done only what she had told him to do.

By trying to obtain children through Hagar, Sarai showed her lack of trust and belief in God. The Lord had promised her husband a child, and she had been determined to make it come to pass one way or another. Her desire for a child became all-consuming—and it came between her and God. In addition, she endangered her husband's trust in the Lord. As Brueggemann observes, Abraham's son Ishmael "is a temptation for Abraham to trust in the fruit of his own work rather than in [God's] promise (cf. Gen. 17:18). . . . [The apostle] Paul has seen correctly that . . . Hagar and Ishmael function as an alternative to the promise."[5]

Hagar Runs Away

Sarai dealt "harshly" with Hagar to the point that the servant took the desperate action of running away. Because people could survive only in family groups and not alone, running away was a last-ditch measure. The Hebrew word translated "harshly" *(ana)* means "oppressing." Genesis 15:13 and Exodus 1:12 employ the same verb to describe Egyptian abuse of the Israelites. The use of the verb here suggests that the narrator disapproved of Sarai's behavior.[6]

Hagar fled into the wilderness and paused at one of its rare springs. Then the "angel of the Lord" spoke to her (Gen. 16:7). The Hebrew word translated "angel" means "messenger" and can apply either to supernatural or human agents. The Old Testament often described "the angel of the Lord" in ways that implied divinity. For example, when Moses encountered the angel of the Lord at the burning bush, the narrator alternately referred to the being as "angel" and "the Lord" ("Yahweh"), implying that they were one and the same. God was the angel here.

"Hagar, slave-girl of Sarai, where have you come from and where are you going?" God asked (verse 8). Since He knew her by name it would seem that He would also know why she was in the desert. Apparently she needed to acknowledge what she was doing—running away. Then the Lord told her to return and submit to her mistress (verse 9). As He did with Abram, He directed her to make a journey. And He also included a promise that echoed what He had said to Abram: "I will so greatly multiply your offspring that they cannot be counted for the multitude" (verse 10; cf. Gen. 12:2; 15:5).

God announced that the slave girl would bear a son that she would name Ishmael ("God knows"), because "the Lord has given heed to your affliction" (Gen. 16:11). Then He described the character of her son (verse 12). But not only would Hagar name her son—she now names God: "You are El-roi" (verse 13). Verse 13 is the only time in the Old Testament that a human being gives a name to God. Interestingly, Hagar speaks only when she is in the wilderness (cf. Gen. 21:16). She is mute around Abram and Sarai. But once in the wilderness she becomes a person of her own.[7]

Hagar returned to Abram's camp and bore him a son. The patriarch was 86 years old (verses 15, 16), and the author has him naming the child (cf. verse 11), perhaps because society usually considered the father as having authority over such matters.

Symbolic Covenant

Thirteen years later God appeared again to Abram. He once more made a covenant with the patriarch, but in reality it was actually the second stage of what we could regard as a single covenant. The ritual in Genesis 15 asked nothing of Abram but that he totally trust in God's promise. Now the Lord provided him opportunity to demonstrate that belief in concrete action. Going beyond Abram's individual response, the new ritual showed that His covenant with the patriarch also had corporate or community implications. The combined stages portrayed "the inward faith and the outward seal (cf. Rom. 4:9, 11); imputed righteousness and expressed devotion (Gen. 15:6; 17:1)."[8]

For the third time the Lord promised that Abram would be the ancestor of many nations and that he would receive the land of Canaan (Gen. 17:1-8). As a reminder of that promise, He changes his name from Abram ("exulted ancestor") to Abraham (apparently intended to be understood as "ancestor of a multitude") (verse 5). In addition, the Lord renamed Sarai Sarah (verse 15). The ancients considered names to have inherent power in them. A name contained the essence of what something was. By changing the couples' names, God indicated what they would become as He fulfilled His covenant promise. Also, ancient rulers would demonstrate their authority by giving vassals new names, as we see frequently throughout the Old Testament.

God's covenant with Abraham would be an eternal one (verses 7, 13). As a visible symbol of it the Lord chose the rite of circumcision (verses 10-14). Circumcision has been a widespread practice both in ancient and modern cultures, usually to indicate passage into manhood. But God ordered it performed on the male infants. Instead of its being a demonstration of adult endurance, the 8-day-old child was a passive recipient. The covenant was a gift, not something earned. The rite would distinguish God's people from many of the surrounding cultures. All those who wished to join God's people—even if they were not biological descendants of Abraham—could join the covenant community by accepting the rite (verses 12, 13). It would continually remind them of who they were. Rejecting it would cut a person off from the community (verse 14).

God's covenant with Abraham has no known parallel in the ancient world. The nearest thing to it are stories in which a king might restore a god's sanctuary or image and the deity would bless the ruler. But here God establishes the covenant relationship on His own initiative and for His own purposes.

When God announced Sarai's new name, He stated that she would bear a son (verse 16). The thought of a 100-year-old man fathering a child by a 90-year-old woman seemed so incredulous that Abraham instinctively laughed (verse 17). He tried to steer God into something more reasonable and plausible by having Him accept Ishmael as Abraham's promised heir (verse 18). The Lord rejected the request (verse 19), though not because the son by Hagar was in any way inferior. As we shall see, God loved him just as much. An elderly man may be able to impregnate a woman, but a woman far past menopause cannot conceive. The son of promise would be a demonstration of divine power, not human fecundity. The next year Sarah would bear a child that Abraham would name Isaac (verses 19, 21). As for Ishmael, he too would be the ancestor of a great nation (verse 20)—but it would not be the covenant one.

Abraham immediately fulfilled the command to have all the males of his household circumcised (verses 23-27).

Divine Visitors

One day Abraham sat in the shade just inside his tent. Its goatskin roof would shelter him from the sun, and the breeze blowing through the open sides would provide a little cooling. Glancing up, he saw three men standing in front of him. "My lord, if I find favor with you," he told their apparent leader, "do not pass by your servant" (Gen. 18:3). He urged them to wash their feet of the dust of travel and then to rest in the shade of one of the oak trees surrounding his encampment.

Hospitality was a fundamental principle of ancient Near Eastern society. The theme of hospitality runs throughout the book of Genesis. In a world without motels, restaurants, and highway police to protect those journeying along on the roads, the only security that travelers had was the hospitality of those they encountered. Custom required that when someone approached a household, its inhabitants should offer them food and allow them to rest. (Even today in many cultures food establishes a temporary bond between strangers.) By accepting the meal, travelers placed themselves under the protection of the host. The host must safeguard the visitor no matter what the danger.

The importance and significance of meals in biblical culture is why Scripture mentions them so frequently. Scott Bartchy succinctly summarized the role of meals in the ancient Mediterranean world when he wrote, "Being welcomed at a table for the purpose of eating food with another person had become a ceremony richly symbolic of friendship, intimacy and unity. Thus betrayal or unfaithfulness toward anyone with whom one had shared the table was viewed as particularly reprehensible. On the other hand, when persons were estranged, a meal invitation opened the way to reconciliation. Even everyday mealtimes were highly complex events in which social values, boundaries, statuses, and hierarchies were reinforced."[9]

Abraham told his visitors that he would give them "a little bread" (verse 5). But custom demanded that the meal be more extravagant than first promised. The patriarch directed his servants to butcher a calf. A herder's flock was the household's wealth. Sheep and cattle were like stocks and bonds. Eating meat was literally consuming the family wealth. Thus people served it only on rare and special occasions, and because of the lack of refrigeration or other means of preserving a butchered animal, it had to be eaten quickly and shared with friends and neighbors. As for the bread, Abraham's baking used three seahs of flour (about 20 quarts). He provided a banquet for his guests and personally served it under a tree (verse 8).

Perhaps because of a custom that men and women did not eat together (especially if nonfamily males were present), Sarah remained inside the tent. But she would naturally be listening to the conversation. The Lord asked Abraham where his wife was (verse 9). Then the divine visitor announced that when He returned she would have a son (verse 10). Overhearing the comment, Sarah, as did Abraham earlier, laughed at the implausibility of her getting pregnant. After all, she had already gone through menopause (verses 11, 12).

God confronted Abraham about her reaction. "Is anything too wonderful for the Lord?" He challenged the patriarch. Again the Lord repeated that when He returned (at least nine months later) Sarah would have borne a son (verse 14).

The three visitors resumed their journey toward Sodom, and as a good host, Abraham accompanied them for a ways. From their vantage point in the hill country they could see the Dead Sea below and the cities clustered by it as they walked along. Then God broke the silence. "Shall I hide from Abraham what I am about to do, seeing that Abraham shall become a great and mighty nation, and all the nations of the earth shall be blessed in him? No, for I have chosen him, that he may charge his children and his household after him to keep the way of the Lord by doing righteousness and justice" (verses 17-19).

Perhaps the Lord sought to provide a learning experience for Abraham, to create in the human being an empathy with Him to help him catch a sense of the pain He suffered when humanity rebelled and slipped into self-destructive depravity. Even more than that, He always seeks to involve human beings in His deeds. He takes us seriously.

"How great is the outcry against Sodom and Gomorrah and how very grave their sin!" He startled Abraham by announcing, "I must go down and see whether they have done altogether according to the outcry that has come to me; and if not, I will know" (verses 20, 21). As in the Tower of Babel story, the biblical author used the imagery of a judge investigating before rendering a decision. In both cases God sought to demonstrate the fairness of divine justice.

When Abraham learned what God had in mind, he protested. Fearlessly he asked, "Will you indeed sweep away the righteous with the wicked?" (verse 23). Almost all ancients imagined their gods as arbitrary and capricious. In the manner of human beings, divine beings would lie, cheat, steal, and murder to get what they wanted. But Abraham envisioned His God as an ethical and moral being. Yahweh's stated intent violated the patriarch's understanding of how he expected the Lord to behave. "Suppose there are fifty righteous within the city; will you then sweep away the place, and not forgive it for the fifty righteous who are in it?" Abraham asked (verse 24). For Yahweh to punish the innocent along with the guilty contradicted his entire experience with his God. "Far be it from you to do such a thing," he exclaimed twice. "Shall not the Judge of all the earth do what is just?" (verse 25).

The Lord promised to spare Sodom if it did have 50 righteous individuals dwelling in it. But Abraham was not content with that. Becoming even bolder, he continued to bargain with God. Eventually they settled on a minimum figure of 10.[10] God would not destroy the city if it had at least that many righteous people in it. And in the process Abraham had begun to sense a little more both about the fairness of God's actions and also how He valued even a few people.

While observing that haggling is fundamental to all Middle Eastern negotiation, Walton and Matthews comment that Abraham's dialogue with God about the number of righteous individuals "provides a repeated demonstration of God's just actions. A just God will not destroy the righteous without warning or investigation. Even the unrighteous, in this early period, can be spared for the sake of the righteous. On the other hand, however, justice is not served by overlooking wickedness. The discussion of the number of righteous people may not concern whether they can balance the wickedness of the rest but whether, given time, they might be able to exert a reforming influence." [11]

Destruction of Sodom

Archaeologists have not been able to identify the "cities of the plain" with any specific location. [12] They have found, however, evidence that fairly large populations once inhabited the arid region. The people mined the salt, bitumen, and potash deposits, and caravans following the north/south road through the Dead Sea region used its cities as trading centers.

Genesis 13:12 reported that Lot had moved his tent as far as Sodom. But by Genesis 19:2, 3, he had abandoned tent dwelling and was living in a house in Sodom itself. The two angels find him sitting in the gateway of the city. Ancient cities utilized the space around gates as public areas. Merchants conducted business and community courts held legal hearings there. "Sitting in the gate" is a common biblical idiom for being involved in public service or similar activities. By now Lot had become a recognized though still suspect part of Sodom's community life. Again we find the theme of hospitality—or lack of it. Here it includes not only food and lodging but also protection from danger.

When Lot saw the angels in the guise of human beings, he offered them the traditional staples of ancient hospitality (Gen. 19:2). They demurred, saying that they would spend the night in the city square, but Lot insisted "strongly," perhaps because he was aware of the danger from the local inhabitants. Finally they accepted and joined him in a feast (verses 2, 3). The fact that the angels did not immediately accept his hospitality, as was customary, suggested that they might be testing him.

Before the household could retire, the male population of Sodom demanded that Lot send the visitors out to them (verses 4, 5). He had a clear idea of what they had in mind, and tried to reason with them (verses 6, 7).

Lot may have compromised in many ways, but he still upheld the sacredness of hospitality. Unfortunately, though, he offered his daughters to the mob as a substitute for his guests. The influence of life in Sodom had warped his understanding even of hospitality. "He is willing to sacrifice his most precious possessions to uphold his honor by protecting his guests."[13] Only the obstinacy of the mob and the intervention of the angels saved him and his daughters from the consequences of his decision.

Although Lot had managed to work his way into the city's social structure, its inhabitants still regarded him as an outsider (verse 9). The depraved mob was determined to break into Lot's house and seize the strangers. The angels pulled him inside and shut the door, then struck the mob with blindness.[14]

Abraham had bargained with God not to destroy Sodom if it had a nucleus of at least 10 righteous people. Sadly, it did not. The city now faced annihilation. The angels had come to save Lot and his family, however, and they told him to gather any who were willing to leave (verses 12, 13). Lot attempted to convince his prospective sons-in-law, but they thought he was jesting (verse 14). Finally, at dawn, the angels urged him to take his wife and two daughters and to flee (verse 15). But he had become too much a part of Sodom and "lingered" (verse 16). The angels literally had to drag them away by the hand, an action that the biblical account regards as "the Lord being merciful to him" (verse 16). Once outside the city, his divine rescuers ordered them to flee without stopping or looking back lest they be consumed in the disaster (verse 17).

But Lot protested, "Oh, no, my lords, your servant has found favor with you, and you have shown me great kindness in saving my life; but I cannot flee to the hills, for fear the disaster will overtake me and I die" (verses 18, 19). Either he did not trust that God would save him—even after the miraculous intervention he had already experienced—or he was seeking an excuse to stay in the area. Pointing in the direction of a nearby town, he bargained with his rescuers. "Look, that city is near enough to flee to, and it is a little one." By implication he meant that it was not as large as Sodom and thus not as deserving of destruction. He would be safe there (verse 20).

Audacious as his request might be, the angels granted it. They promised that nothing would harm Zoar (the name means "little" [verse 21]). Then the spokesangel explained that he could not destroy Sodom until Lot reached safety (verse 22). Lot should have known that if God had sent His angels to rescue him, He would do everything possible to protect him. The man's worries about his safety were, if nothing else, implied doubts about God's power and intention. He had already shown his lack of faith in God when he had chosen to abandon the Promised Land for the cities of the plain. It meant that he had not been willing to accompany Abraham in his uncle's journey with God. Derek Kidner comments that we can all see ourselves as potential Lots, "lingering, quibbling . . . wheedling a last concession as he is dragged to safety. Not even brimstone will make a pilgrim of him: he must have his little Sodom again if life is to be supportable." [15]

Lot's wife perished in Sodom's destruction because she ignored the warning not to look back (verse 26; cf. verse 17). Commentators often explain that she valued her former home more than God's command to flee. But she was only reflecting the attitude that her husband had so long modeled. He might not have physically glanced back as she did, but his mind was still staring over his shoulder at Sodom.

But something even worse than his wife's death would happen to him. Afraid to stay in Zoar, Lot left and settled in the hills. The man who had once had an impressive house now lived in a cave (verse 30). His daughters, terrified that they would be left childless in a culture that valued women primarily as mothers, tricked him into impregnating them (verses 31-36). The father who would have let others dishonor his daughters to uphold a perverted concept of hospitality now found himself shamed by those same daughters as they sought to fulfill their culture's obsession for maintaining a family line. Like Sarah, they decided to obtain the divine promise of children through their own efforts. And their decision would have drastic consequences. Their descendants, especially the Moabites and the Ammonites, would become hostile rivals of the promised heir.

The story of Lot and Sodom is an example of the biblical love of patterns. It echoes the story of Noah, in which one family is divinely saved from destruction, then the drunken father gets disgraced by his children (cf. Gen. 9:20-27). Lot's frustrated attempt to offer hospitality is also a distorted reflection of the earlier account of Abram as host. Abram's story ends in Sarai's pregnancy of the promised son, while Lot's tale concludes with the incestuous pregnancies of his daughters.

---

[1] J. H. Hellerman, *The Ancient Church as Family*, p. 32.

[2] As scholars translated clay tablets found at an ancient city in northeastern Iraq known as Nuzi, they discovered that the documents depicted many practices that appeared similar to those in the Abraham story, including wife-sister relationships, adoption of a family slave

as heir to a childless couple, and taking a secondary wife. For a time scholars used the parallels to date Abraham's lifetime. More recent scholars are more cautious in applying the parallels directly, but the tablets do help us better understand ancient culture. For a brief overview of how the Nuzi documents illuminate the Bible, see Tremper Longman III, *How to Read Genesis,* pp. 88, 89.

[3] J. H. Walton and V. H. Matthews, *The IVP Bible Background Commentary: Genesis to Deuteronomy,* p. 42.

[4] In Genesis 16:1-6 Sarai recognizes Abram as head of the household, but he listens to her suggestion about Hagar. His headship was not autocratic.

[5] Walter Brueggemann, *Genesis* (Atlanta: John Knox Press, 1982), p. 152.

[6] Daniel I. Block, "Marriage and Family in Ancient Israel," in *Marriage and Family in the Biblical Word,* ed. K. M. Campbell, p. 77.

[7] Gina Hens-Piazza, *Nameless, Blameless, and Without Shame: Two Cannibal Mothers Before a King* (Collegeville, Minn.: Liturgical Press, 2003), p. 107.

[8] Derek Kidner, *Genesis: An Introduction and Commentary* (Downers Grove, Ill.: Inter-Varsity Press, 1967), p. 128.

[9] Cited in Hellerman, p. 85.

[10] In a biblical world a major city might have only a few hundred inhabitants.

[11] Walton and Matthews, p. 46.

[12] Some archaeologists identify Sodom with the modern site of Bab edh-Dhra. The Smithsonian Institute has excavated its ruins and displays a reconstructed tomb and the faces of its people in its Natural History Museum in Washington, D.C.

[13] Walton and Matthews, p. 46.

[14] Kidner suggests that the word translated "blindness" here may indicate a dazzled state, as the Old Testament elsewhere associates it with angels (2 Kings 6:18) (p. 134).

[15] *Ibid.,* p. 135.

9

"Sacrifice Your Only Son"
Genesis 20:1-25:18

Abraham had apparently learned little from his experience in Egypt. He was still afraid that some powerful elite would seize Sarah as a wife and have him killed. Again, when he settled in Gerar, he instructed her to pass herself off as a sister (Gen. 20:2). And she was still willing to go along with the ploy. For whatever his reason, the local ruler did take her as a wife. God then sent a dream to Abimelech. It was a widespread belief in the ancient Near East that the gods communicated with human beings through such dreams. The Lord employed dreams here with Abimelech and later with Pharaoh and Nebuchadnezzar. (However, He rarely spoke to Israelites through them.)

In the dream God told Abimelech that he was about to die because he had taken Sarah. The pagan ruler protested, declaring that he had not touched Abraham's wife. It was not fair for Abraham's God to destroy him and his people when the couple had clearly claimed to be brother and sister. He was innocent of wrongdoing (verses 3-5). In response God acknowledged that the king had not yet done anything—in fact, He had prevented the ruler from "sinning against me" (verse 6). But he must return Abraham's wife, and her husband must pray for Abimelech. God described Abraham as a prophet whom He would have intercede with Him for the king. If the ruler did keep Sarah, though, he and his household would perish (verse 7).

This time when a pagan ruler demanded to know why Abraham had deceived him, the patriarch attempted to excuse himself. "I did it because

I thought, There is no fear of God at all in this place, and they will kill me because of my wife" (verse 11). Yet the king did show "fear," or respect, for Abraham's God—perhaps even more than the patriarch did sometimes. Abraham also tried to justify his ruse because Sarah really was his sister. In a way he put some of the blame for his actions on God Himself. If the Lord had not told him to leave his home, Abraham would not have had to hide behind a facade to protect himself (verses 10-13).

Unlike Pharaoh, Abimelech did not expel Abraham. He invited him to settle in his territory (verses 14, 15). But like the Egyptian king, he gave great gifts to Abraham, including 1,000 shekels (about 25 pounds of silver in the form of bars or rings). It was more than a laborer would ever earn in a lifetime. In Ugaritic mythology it was the price the gods paid for their brides. When Abimelech told Sarah that he had given "your brother" (verse 17) the money, he seemed to accept Abraham's explanation, duplicitous though it may be in the reader's eye. God had prevented the king's wife and female slaves from bearing children. The ancient world regarded disease or similar problems as the result of displeasing a god or other supernatural power, and the God of Abraham may have allowed the temporary infertility because it was something that the Canaanite ruler believed in and would thus would have taken seriously. Abraham prayed for Abimelech's family, and they began to conceive again (verses 17, 18)—and so did Sarah.

She bore a son and named him Isaac ("laughter"). "God has brought laughter for me; everyone who hears will laugh with me" (Gen. 21:6). Sarah had laughed at God's promise that she would have a child. Now she laughs from a different emotion after giving birth.

Expulsion of Ishmael

Unfortunately, another kind of laughter eventually tore Abraham's family apart. During the feast to celebrate Isaac's weaning, Sarah spotted Ishmael "playing" with Isaac (verse 9), and she became extremely upset. Many commentators interpret the passage as indicating that Ishmael was "mocking"[1] his younger half brother as the cause. Some others see the fact that Ishmael regarded himself as an equal as what disturbed her. Whatever the reason, she demanded that Abraham get rid of "the slave woman" and "her son." She vowed that Ishmael would never inherit along with Isaac (verse 10). Her ultimatum devastated Abraham (verse 11), but God told him to do as his wife wanted (verse 12).

The narrator stressed both Abraham's and God's concern for Hagar and her son. The Lord reassured Abraham that Ishmael's departure was necessary for the fulfillment of His promise to Abraham and Sarah about a son of their own. The patriarch took care of Hagar and Ishmael's needs before he sent them away. Sarah wanted her slave "cast out" *(gares)* (verse 10). But Abraham "sent" *(silleah)* her away. *Silleah* is often used when someone dispatches an agent to fulfill a mission.[2]

Scholars have noticed many interesting parallels between the story of Hagar and that of Moses. In many ways Scripture has presented her as a proto-Moses. For example, both flee oppression into the desert and come to a well (Gen. 16:6, 7, 14; Ex. 2:15). Both encounter God (Gen. 16:13; Ex. 3). Moses learns the name of God (Ex. 3:14), while Hagar goes beyond Moses to name the deity (Gen. 16:13). The Lord tells both of them to return to the oppression they had escaped from (verse 9; Ex. 3:10). Eventually they were expelled from their bondage back into the desert (Gen. 21:10-14; Ex. 12:31-33). In the desert God delivered them from death, particularly from thirst (Gen. 21:15-19; Ex. 14; 15:22-25; 17). And both became heads of a great people consisting of 12 tribes (Gen. 16:10; 21:18; 25:12-16; Num. 1). God cared just as much for Ishmael and his descendants as He did for Isaac and his future offspring. After all, the Lord had promised Abram that he would be "the ancestor of a multitude of nations" (Gen. 17:5).

Covenant With Abimelech

After his previous experience with Abraham, Abimelech was naturally rather cautious toward the patriarch. Acknowledging that Abraham's God sided with the alien pastoralist,[3] he asked him not to deal deceptively with him or his offspring. Abimelech had dealt honestly with Abraham, and he now requested that the patriarch respond in kind. Abraham vowed that he would (Gen. 21:22-24). But a situation soon arose that would test their relationship (and by implication, Abraham's character).

The local ruler's men seized a well that Abraham's servants had dug. Abraham complained to Abimelech,[4] who denied any knowledge of the incident (verses 25, 26). The patriarch brought him seven ewe lambs. When Abimelech asked about their significance, Abraham replied that by accepting them the ruler would "be a witness for me that I dug this well" (verse 30). By taking them, the ruler made a covenant with Abraham. But, as the narrator reminds us, the patriarch was still only an alien resident in the Promised Land (verse 34).

The Command to Sacrifice the Son of Promise

Some time later God did one of His strangest and most troubling actions in Scripture: He commanded Abraham to offer Isaac as a burnt offering on a mountain in the land of Moriah (Gen. 22:1, 2). Bible writers do not often make editorial comments or inject themselves into what they write. Rarely do they give background information or comment on a story. Fokkelman observes that the biblical author "wants to make us think, and the best way to do this is to speak indirectly and implicitly."[5] But when they do make a clear statement, it is extremely important, and we must pay careful attention to it. Here the author immediately tells the point of the story—that it is only a test, thus lessening the shock of God's command and protecting His character. The reader now knows something that Abraham does not. Even then, though, the divine command is abrupt and still startling.

Scripture does not reveal the point of the ordeal. Through the centuries people have struggled to explain its intent. A traditional Jewish commentary, for example, offers a number of suggestions, ranging from the test's being a punishment for Abraham's making a covenant with Abimelech about land that God had already promised the patriarch to its giving Abraham an opportunity to put his potential goodness into concrete action.[6] By not explaining God's reason for the command, Scripture also makes the story a test for the reader. Are we willing, it asks us, to trust God just as Abraham did? Furthermore, the biblical author allows the reader to view the incident from many different perspectives. We can keep going back to the text again and again to find additional understandings.

The phrase "your only son Isaac" (verse 2) repeats and stresses the themes of childlessness and divine promise. In Genesis 12:1 God had told Abram to "go forth." Now in Genesis 22:2 He again requests him to "go forth." He sends the patriarch on still another journey that will test his obedience and trust even more than the first one. Rising early in the morning, Abraham set out with Isaac, two servants, and a load of firewood for the burnt offering (verse 3).

Human sacrifice, especially of the firstborn, was a familiar concept to the ancient world. No sacrifice could be more powerful. The pharaohs depicted their conquests in Canaan on temple walls. In one of them the Egyptian forces have besieged a city. On top of the city wall stands its ruler about to hurl his son down to the ground. Surely, he reasons, his god must deliver his people after such an ultimate sacrifice.

Abraham had bargained with God to prevent the destruction of Sodom, but to our surprise he said nothing to Him when the Lord asked him to sacrifice his son. The patriarch has grown immensely in his relationship with his God. He is now willing to do whatever the Lord asks of him without resorting to his own strategies, such as passing off Sarah as his sister. "Noteworthy is the way the narrative excessively and deliberately details Abraham's preparations for the journey and the journey itself. Without explicit commentary, we are left to ponder the thoughts of Abraham as he so matter-of-factly carries out God's directions. When at last someone in the narrative speaks, it is Isaac, not God, who breaks the silence, and the question he raises serves only to heighten the anguish of the Lord's request."[7] The story leaves its readers to wonder how they would react if they were in Abraham's sandals.

After Isaac pointed out the lack of an offering, Abraham said that God would provide it—not "You're it." When Abraham reached the place that God revealed as where he should sacrifice his son, the patriarch told his servants, "Stay here with the donkey; the boy and I will go over there; we will worship, and then we will come back to you" (Gen. 22:5). He states explicitly that he and Isaac would return.

Paintings and other illustrations usually depict Isaac as still a child at this point. Fokkelman suggests that since the highly structured story of Abraham has a gap of 13 years between Genesis 16:16 and Genesis 17:1, the author implies the same time period between Isaac's birth and that of Genesis 22.[8] Isaac, by now in his teens, could have easily overpowered and escaped his elderly father. But Abraham's son trusted him and accompanied him. Twice the passage mentions that father and son walked together (Gen. 22:6, 8), impressing on the reader the image of their going willingly with each other.

Abraham constructed an altar and arranged the firewood. He bound his son as a priest would a sacrificial animal[9] and laid him on the wood. Still the narrator gives no hint of what might be going through Abraham's mind. The author is interested only in that the patriarch obeys. Just as Abraham raised the knife[10] to slay his son, the angel of the Lord called the father's name. Abraham answered (verse 11). The Lord told him not to harm the boy, because "now I know that you fear God, since you have not withheld your son, your only son, from me" (verse 12). Abraham had demonstrated that his loyalty to God was even stronger than the ancient world's most powerful human tie: that to one's bloodline.

Both here and in verse 2 God referred to Isaac as "your only son," not in the sense that Abraham had no other children (he had Ishmael) but that Isaac was the son of promise. The lad was God's special gift to him. The divine summons for Abraham to sacrifice his son not only depicts a test of the man's obedience, but again emphasizes the theme that the true son comes only by miraculous means. Ironically, Abraham "has retained his son only by renouncing him."[11]

Glancing up from Isaac, Abraham noticed a ram caught by its horns in a thicket. He instantly realized that it was his substitute offering for his son (verse 13).[12] After the sacrifice the patriarch named the place "The Lord will provide" (verse 14). The Lord had provided more than just a sacrifice. Abraham's God had given him a son and held out a wondrous future for that young man's descendants.

The angel of the Lord now once again repeated that promise. He would bless Abraham and "make your offspring as numerous as the stars of heaven and as the sand that is on the seashore" (verse 17). But the blessing was not for Abraham and his descendants alone. As in the initial call, they would be a channel of blessing for all nations on earth, because "you have obeyed my voice" (verse 18).

The Burial Cave of Machpelah

Sarah died, and her husband mourned her (Gen. 23:2). But the biblical author is more interested in where she would be buried than in her death. As a resident alien, Abraham's clan had no cemetery of its own. Approaching the local Hittites, he asked for a place to shelter his household's dead (verse 4). The Hittites, regarding him as "a mighty prince" (verse 6), that is, the leader of a large and influential household, offered him his choice of burial grounds. But Abraham had one particular site in mind. He requested that the Hittite leaders persuade Ephron son of Zohar to sell him the cave of Machpelah (verses 7-9). Abraham's family would bury their dead in the cave until the bodies disintegrated, then collect the bones in a pile.

Displaying typically extravagant Near Eastern generosity, Ephron offered the site to Abraham as a gift, but the patriarch purchased it at full price. If he had not, Ephron's heirs could have reclaimed it. And to have paid a lesser price could have allowed Ephron's family to consider the difference between the recognized value and the actual purchase price as a debt that Abraham's family still owed. Again Ephron's heirs would have had an excuse to get the land back. Abraham wanted the little piece of land to belong to his descendants without any question. The transaction took place in what archaeological evidence suggests was a massive gate and tower complex.[13] He paid about seven and a quarter pounds of silver for the cave. The patriarch now legally owned a piece of Canaan. The burial site would be a token that someday all the land would belong to Abraham's descendants. It was also near Mamre, where Abraham had received many of his promises from God (Gen. 13:18; 18:1).

A Wife for Isaac

Abraham was concerned that his son avoid alliances with Canaanite women. He was sure that God would provide Isaac a suitable wife. "Experience had taught him that the God of heaven and earth would see to his promise articulated at Abraham's call and reiterated at decisive stages in the patriarch's pilgrimage."[14] The patriarch commissioned his chief servant, or steward, to go to Abraham's kin in Mesopotamia to find a wife for his son (Gen. 24:1-9). The servant asked what he should do if the prospective bride refused to come back with him to Canaan. Must he take Isaac to Abraham's ancestral homeland (verse 5)? His master immediately rejected the idea (verses 6-8). To do that would be to nullify God's call to Abraham. The last recorded words of Abraham in Scripture recount God's leading and promises for his life and how his descendants must continue this trusting relationship (verses 6-8).

Leading a caravan of 10 camels loaded with gifts, the servant set out for the city of Aram-naharaim, home of Abraham's relative Nahor. After arriving at evening, the steward made the camels kneel. He shared his master's faith in Abraham's God. Now he prayed that the Lord would give him success in his mission. "Let the girl to whom I shall say, 'Please offer your jar that I may drink,' and who shall say, 'Drink, and I will water your camels'— let her be the one whom you have appointed for your servant Isaac. By this I shall know that you have shown steadfast love to my master" (verse 14).

Even before he finished his prayer, Rebekah, Abraham's niece, approached the spring or well. She filled her jar and hoisted it upon her shoulder. Abraham's servant ran to her and requested a sip of water. She gave him a drink, then offered to water his camels (verses 15-20). A thirsty camel can drink as much as 25 gallons. The water jar that Rebekah used to fill the watering trough would have probably held no more than three gallons, and it would have taken her a long time to satisfy the thirsty animals. The servant stared at her in silence, wondering if God had now fulfilled his mission (verse 21).

After Rebekah finished with the camels, the servant inquired who she was and whether her family had room for him and his caravan to spend the night (verses 22-25). When he learned her identity, the man responded in awe and worship (verses 26, 27).

The girl raced home to tell her family what had just happened. Her brother, Laban, instantly spotted the gold nose-ring and heavy bracelets Abraham's servant had given her. Laban immediately began to exhibit the characteristics of greed and opportunism that would be so prominent in the Jacob stories. He hurried to the spring, found Abraham's servant, and invited him to his home. But the servant would not accept food until he had explained his mission.

Again we see an example of the biblical love of themes and literary patterns. Here the author has the servant echo the call of Abraham. "In [Genesis] 24:1, 35-36 we learn that, in accord with his promise in 12:2, Yahweh has blessed Abraham with long years, great wealth, and a son. The verb 'bless' is a key word in this chapter, occurring in vv. 1, 27, 31, 35, 48, and 60. God's command 'Go!' to the patriarch in 12:1 is complemented by Rebekah's 'I will go' in 24:58 (and her family's 'she will go' in v. 55). In 12:1, Yahweh commands Abraham to leave 'your land and your kinsfolk and the house of your father.' In chap. 24, the same expression occurs in whole or in part in vv. 4, 7, 38, and 40. Yahweh's promise to Abraham in 12:2 ('I will make your name great') is repeated in his servant's words in v. 35 ('Yahweh has blessed my master exceedingly and he has become great')." [15]

Abraham's servant also recognized Laban's character. By stressing his master's wealth and Isaac's sole heirship (Gen. 24:35, 36), he knew that Laban would favor the union of the two households. The servant also emphasized Abraham's desire to marry a close relative instead of a Canaanite (verses 37-41) and that his encounter with Rebekah at the well had been an answer to prayer. For many reasons Laban cannot reject the marriage offer (verses 50, 51).

Although the family initially accepted the proposal, they began stalling the next day (verse 55).[16] The servant wanted to return to Canaan immediately. Perhaps hoping that Rebekah herself would postpone her departure, the mother and brother asked her what she wanted to do. To their disappointment, she was willing to go at once (verses 54-59). When she left, her family gave her a parting blessing that echoed God's blessing to Abraham (verse 60; cf. Gen. 22:17).

Genesis 24:62 has Isaac coming from Beer-lahai-roi, the place where Hagar met God and He told her that she would be the mother of a nation. Isaac glanced up and saw the mother of his own nation approaching. When she spotted him, she immediately slid off her camel and asked Abraham's servant who the man coming toward them was. Learning his identity, she veiled herself, a symbol of her marriage to him. The servant explained the successful completion of his mission to his master's son, and Isaac took Rebekah into Sarah's tent, which had remained empty since his mother's death. The act signified that she was the new mistress of the household.

Patterns in Genesis

Genesis 12-24 have formed a ring or concentric cycle of stories in which the first and last units of the literary structure echo each other, the second and next-to-last units parallel, and so forth. Or to put it another way, the passage follows a certain sequence, then reverses itself, the second half becoming a mirror image of the first.[17] Many times the midpoint of such a literary structure will contain the main point of the story (biblical writers put the climax in the middle of a story instead of the end, as modern authors do). Such ring or concentric patterns are one of the main literary devices used by biblical writers. They link the various stories and keep reminding us of God's working in both human history and individual lives. The biblical writers used them to emphasize the main points of a story as well as a memorization aid for people who knew the story only orally. The pattern will repeat itself again and again, as in the Jacob story later. Because Scripture presents much of its message in such stylistic devices, the reader must be alert for them to hear all that the author has to say.

In Genesis 12-24 Abraham leaves on a quest for land and seeks some kind of heir, whether it be the adoption of a trusted servant or the fathering of a son through a secondary wife (Gen. 15; 16). The "climax" comes in Genesis 17-21, which relates God's covenant with Abraham and the birth of Isaac. Genesis 22 has Abraham nearly losing the son he has sought for so long, and Genesis 23 and 24 has, among other things, the patriarch purchasing land for a burial place (a symbol of the whole land his descendants will acquire) and Isaac marrying Rebekah, thus passing on the covenant to the next generation.

The Death of Abraham

Abraham had other sons (Gen. 25:1-6).[18] As he did with Ishmael, he sends them away from Isaac. The inheritance went exclusively to Isaac. Genesis lists the sons through Keturah here first (since the narrative presents them last), Isaac in the middle (the most important position in Hebrew literary style), and Ishmael last (since he appeared in the Abraham cycle of stories first).

Eventually Abraham died, and Isaac and Ishmael buried him with Sarah in the cave of Machpelah (verses 7-10). God then focused His blessing on Isaac. But He did not forget Ishmael and His promise to Hagar (verses 12-18). Ishmael was also a beloved son.

---

[1] The Hebrew has a wordplay on Isaac's name (D. Kidner, *Genesis,* p. 140).

[2] D. I. Block, in *Marriage and Family in the Biblical World,* ed. K. M. Campbell, p. 77.

[3] The biblical narrator echoes this in Genesis 26:28; 30:27; and 39:3.

[4] The Hebrew word the author uses here implies that Abraham may have had to protest several times. The dispute about the well will surface again in Genesis 26.

[5] J. Fokkelman, *Reading Biblical Narrative,* p. 149.

[6] *The Soncino Chumash: The Five Books of Moses With Haphtaroth,* ed. A. Cohen (London: Soncino Press, 1983), p. 108.

[7] *Zondervan NIV Bible Commentary,* ed. Kenneth L. Barker and John R. Kohlenberger III (Grand Rapids: Zondervan, 1994), Vol. I, p. 33.

[8] Fokkelman, p. 43.

[9] Jewish tradition refers to this story as "The Binding of Isaac" instead of "The Sacrifice of Isaac."

[10] See Jeffrey R. Chadwick, "Discovering Hebron," *Biblical Archaeology Review,* September/October 2005, p. 30, for a photo of what may have been the kind of knife Abraham might have used.

[11] Fokkelman, p. 164.

[12] Commentators have frequently compared and contrasted the story of Abraham and Isaac with the enigmatic account of Jephthah and his daughter in Judges 11 (see, for example, Barbara Miller, *Tell It on the Mountain: The Daughter of Jephthah in Judges 11* (Collegeville, Minn.: Liturgical Press, 2005), pp. 36-38. Perhaps one important clue to understanding the Jephthah narrative is the fact that the inhabitants of the typical four-room, two-story Israelite house kept their animals inside the lower story (Larry G. Herr and Douglas R. Clark, "Excavating the Tribe of Reuben," *Biblical Archaeology Review,* March/April 2001, pp. 36-47; Michael G. Hasel, "Architecture," in *Eerdmans Dictionary of the Bible,* ed. D. N. Freedman, pp. 96-99; Michael G. Hasel, "House," in *Eerdmans Dictionary of the Bible,* ed. D. N. Freedman, pp. 612, 613). Because he stabled his animals in the lower part of the house, Jephthah would have naturally expected one of them to wander out first when he arrived home. Perhaps he even had in the back of his mind the story of the divinely provided ram of the Abraham narrative.

[13] Chadwick, pp. 28, 29.

[14] James L. Crenshaw, *Samson: A Secret Betrayed, a Vow Ignored* (Atlanta: John Knox Press, 1978), p. 27.

[15] *HarperCollins Bible Commentary,* ed. James L. Mays (San Francisco: HarperSanFrancisco, 2000), p. 97.

[16] The "at least 10 days" could represent a period of up to a year (*Eerdmans Commentary on the Bible,* ed. James D. G. Dunn and John W. Rogerson [Grand Rapids: Eerdmans, 2003], p. 56).

[17] Scholars also refer to these as chiastic structures.

[18] Some commentators suggest that Abraham married Keturah before Sarah's death (perhaps after Hagar left), but the biblical writer does not mention them until now to stress that only Isaac was the child of promise (see Kidner, pp. 149, 150; *Eerdmans Commentary on the Bible,* p. 56).

10

The Supplanter
Genesis 25:19-29:30

Apart from the story of David's sons, the narrative of Jacob and Esau[1] offers the classic example of struggle between brothers for dominance with a family, something that violated one of the most fundamental principles of the biblical world. The symbol of that struggle was the birthright. Most commentators and readers of the Bible focus on what they see as the religious dimensions of the birthright, often limiting the conflict to who would be the ancestor of the Messiah. But the issues were broader than that and would extend to succeeding generations. And it would tear apart Jacob's family simply because of what kind of person he was.

At first Rebekah seemed barren. This is the third time the theme of sterility has appeared in Genesis. It is almost as if God were making the biological continuation of the promised line as difficult as possible, to remind them that He was the one fulfilling the promise. Isaac prayed that she would be able to have children (Gen. 25:21).

When she at last conceived, a set of twins resulted. Babies naturally begin moving within the womb when they reach a certain level of development, as any mother soon learns. But the movements of Rebekah's children were unusual to say the least. In fact, their violent twistings and turnings frightened her. It seemed as if they were fighting each other (verse 22). Scripture took the struggle between the twins so seriously that it portrayed the conflict as beginning before they were even born.

Rebekah sought an explanation from God Himself as to why she did not die in childbirth. Scripture does not explain how she contacted the

Lord, whether through prayer or in some other manner. It just declares that when she inquired of the Lord, He told her in a poem consisting of four half verses:

> "Two nations are in your womb,
> > and two peoples born of you shall be divided;
> the one shall be stronger than the other,
> > the elder shall serve the younger" (verse 23).

The last line would have been startling in the ancient world. The younger always served the older, and the firstborn son had a special place in the family.[2] Birth order determined a son's place in life. Both custom and biblical law gave the firstborn special privileges (cf. Gen. 48:13, 14, 17, 18; Deut. 21:15-17; 2 Chron. 21:3). But Scripture consistently reverses the pattern. And this divine oracle will motivate the actions of mother and younger son from now on.

Although Esau came through the birth canal first, Jacob symbolically displayed his lifelong character by holding on to his brother's heel.[3] In her culture's typical love of wordplay, Rebekah named the second son "Jacob" in allusion to his grasping of his brother's foot. The name did not actually mean "heel"—it just sounded like the Hebrew word.

Esau Sells His Birthright

Esau became a skillful hunter, living out of doors, while Jacob, a quieter personality, spent most of his time around the encampment (Gen. 25:27). He seemed to have been in charge of the family flocks. Each twin was a favorite of one of their parents. Isaac's fondness for wild game attracted him to Esau, and Rebekah was especially close to Jacob (verse 28).

One day as Jacob prepared a stew Esau returned famished from a hunting expedition. "Let me eat some of that red stuff," he begged (verse 30).[4] "First sell me your birthright," Jacob countered (verse 31). "I am about to die; of what use is a birthright to me?" Esau replied (verse 32). The older brother was impulsive and oblivious of future consequences. The younger had a solid streak that quickly became calculating and deceptive. Before Jacob would give his brother any of the lentil stew, he demanded that Esau let him have the birthright in exchange (verse 33). In Israel the birthright had religious implications, including the role of family spiritual leader. At least in other ancient cultures the birthright could be sold or transferred.[5]

The incident probably took place while Isaac was in charge of an en-

116

campment for the family shepherds. Since Isaac would have supervised it, he would have had the authority to make such a decision there. Also the other shepherds would have been able to act as witnesses to the agreement.

Modern readers do not grasp the full significance of the struggle that has now begun between Jacob and Isaac (and will be duplicated among Jacob's sons). The modern Western world considers husband and wife as having the strongest social tie. But in the biblical world and even many cultures still today the most power bonds exist between siblings—brothers and sisters. If one had to make a choice between the demands of a wife or a sibling, sibling relations came first.[6] Jacob's family was dysfunctional not only in a modern sense, but even more so in its own culture.

Another famine struck Canaan, and Isaac was apparently tempted to find refuge in Egypt, as his father had done. God told him not to go but to reside in the territory of Abimelech, and then repeated the promise He had made to his father (Gen. 26:1-5). Isaac settled in Gerar. Families often pass their worst traits from generation to generation, and we see that illustrated here. As had his father, Isaac feared that he would be killed and his wife stolen. The patriarch decided to use the same ruse that his father had employed. He asked the attractive Rebekah to claim to be his sister. But Abimelech discovered the truth when one day he glanced out a window and saw Isaac fondling his wife. Naturally the ruler was upset (verses 6-11).

Deception is a continual theme in the book of Genesis, beginning with Satan in the Garden of Eden. Each generation is as flawed as the previous one. But the Lord does not abandon any of them. In the incidents of Genesis 26 "we see how God's promises made initially to Abraham were even more abundantly fulfilled in the life of Isaac. Once again, this was not always the result of his virtue but happened despite his mistakes. The timid can experience divine blessings as much as those who respond to God's call with greater confidence. Indeed, God's grace is more evident in weaker vessels (1 Cor. 1:27-31; 2 Cor. 4:7)."[7]

The Trickster Emerges

God had told Rebekah that Esau would serve Jacob, but she was not content to let Him work out His prediction in His own way. She decided to help the prophetic fulfillment along. Ancient sources often depict the extent once-barren women went to promote their male children,[8] but Rebekah focused on just one of her sons.

Isaac unwittingly precipitated her intervention through some duplicity of his own. He was determined to give his favorite, Esau, the special blessing. A blessing, which consisted of a promise of favor, was a great honor to the one who received it. "Such blessings were more than good wishes; in some sense they were efficacious in bringing about what the patriarch conferred."[9] Isaac worked out a ploy in which he could bestow it without Rebekah knowing what he was up to until afterward. Yet he would still be able to celebrate the occasion, a vital aspect of any important event.

Summoning Esau to him, he ordered the older brother to hunt him some game and prepare him a meal. Then he would give Esau the special blessing (Gen. 27:1-4). As we saw earlier, the ancients ate little meat because it would have involved using up part of the family wealth. But hunting would have provided some variation in diet without the loss of any of the flock. People celebrated important events with meals. Isaac wanted to honor his giving of the blessing to Esau, so he sent his firstborn out to hunt. Also, by using wild game he would not have to answer any questions from Rebekah about why he wanted to slaughter a precious herd animal. Isaac claimed that he wanted to do it because he did not know when he might die. According to custom, a father was supposed to call all his sons together if it really was a deathbed blessing. But he summoned only Esau. In many ways both sons would soon become victims of a silent struggle between their parents.

Unfortunately, Rebekah overheard Isaac's plan. Perhaps she had kept an eye on everything her husband and Esau did together. Immediately finding her favorite, Jacob, she outlined her own scheme to get the blessing for him. Jacob would bring food to Isaac first and receive the blessing (verses 5-10). Jacob agreed to go along with her, though he did see a problem. Esau had a much more hairy body, and although Isaac's eyesight might have dimmed with age (verse 1), he had not lost his sense of touch. His father might detect the deception and turn the blessing into a curse (verse 12). Rebekah did not care. "Let your curse be on me, my son; only obey my word" (verse 13). Sadly, her words would come true.

Already we have seen a family pattern of deception. Now it intensifies in Abraham's grandson. We could call Jacob a trickster figure, a popular literary type in parts of the world.[10] Many cultures admire the trickster, such as the coyote trickster of North American Indian legends. Scripture does not approve of Jacob's trickster characteristics, but it does not explicitly condemn him. Instead the biblical writer lets us see the consequences of such behavior and then draw our own conclusions.

Meat from wild game would be tough and strong tasting. People would stew such meat to tenderize it, and cook it with herbs and spices to give it a better flavor. Now Rebekah would use such spices to mask the fact that Jacob had brought his father meat from the family flock. Covering her son's arms with animal skins hid his smoother skin.

Rebekah's plan worked, and mother and son tricked Isaac into giving Jacob the special blessing (verses 5-29). The wording of Isaac's blessing echoes the divine oracle that Rebekah received before the twins' birth. It reminds the reader that even when people turn to deception God is still in control. The blessing focuses on fertility and dominion (verses 28, 29). Jacob was able to fool Isaac because of the father's physical blindness. But Isaac's partiality toward Esau had blinded him in other ways. In fact, the entire family was spiritually blind.

Jacob had barely left when Esau arrived and discovered what had happened. Isaac trembled "violently" as he realized that he had given the blessing to the wrong son (verse 33). Esau was devastated (verse 34).[11] He may have treated the honor of the blessing lightly in the past, but now a recognition of what he had lost overwhelmed him as he begged for his father to bless him also (verse 34). People in the biblical world believed that once a blessing or curse had been made, it could not be rescinded. Because of that, Isaac could not see how he could take back what he had already said. But he did bless Esau. Its wording also touched the themes of fertility and dominion, but in a mirror image. Esau would be exiled from the fertility of the land (perhaps echoing the curse of Cain [Gen. 4:12]?) And he would serve Jacob until he broke away (Gen. 27:39, 40). "The feeble substitute for a blessing hardly eased the pain, inasmuch as he was destined to serve his younger brother."[12] Isaac had called Jacob "my son" seven times, but now he applied the term to Esau only once. Had he somehow pulled away emotionally from his favorite son?

Jacob had taken both Esau's birthright and blessing (verse 36). Understandably Esau was furious and vowed revenge. Isaac had implied that he was near death (verse 2). As soon as their father did die, Esau threatened, he would kill his brother once the period of mourning ended (verse 41). Yet Walter Brueggemann notes that in Scripture Jacob's brother "is handled carefully and respectfully all through this narrative."[13] Even though the biblical writer mentioned Esau's anger, he did so "uncritically and not without justification."[14]

Learning of Esau's anger, Rebekah knew that she needed to get Jacob to a safer place until his brother's anger cooled off. She knew that he could stay for a while with her own brother, Laban, in Haran (verses 41-45). But she had to make some kind of excuse to send him there.

People in the ancient world rarely traveled unless they were merchants.

Abraham had dispatched his servant to find a wife lest Isaac marry a Canaanite. Why not use the same reason as a cover for Jacob's visit to Laban? Attacking Esau (and by implication, Isaac), she complained to her husband, "I am weary of my life because of the Hittite women [Esau's wives (Gen. 26:34, 35)]. If Jacob marries one of the Hittite women such as these, one of the women of the land, what good will my life be to me?" (Gen. 27:46).

Jacob continued to receive good training from his mother in the art of trickery and deceit. She had made him into a tool to get the birthright blessing from Isaac. But her scheme instantly placed her favorite son in danger, and she had to get him out of the predicament. Rebekah now manipulated her husband to solve the problem by having him send Jacob to relatives in Paddan-aram. In stealing the birthright, Jacob took an active role. But when through Isaac his mother has him sent to find a wife among the daughters of Laban, Jacob becomes little more than an object controlled by others, a major part of the pattern of his life from now on. For the moment Rebekah may congratulate herself on her successful strategy against Isaac and Esau. But she has tricked one other person even more— herself. Because of it she will never see Jacob again.

Isaac swallowed the ploy and directed Jacob to find a wife among his cousins (Gen. 28:1, 2). Marriage between cousins has long been the ideal in the Middle East. His parting blessing reflected the ones that God had given Abraham (verses 3, 4).[15]

When Esau heard his father tell Jacob not to marry a Canaanite woman, he took it seriously. To make amends, he found another wife from within his extended family. He married a cousin, the daughter of Ishmael. Brueggemann regards the biblical author here as complimenting the older brother.[16] Also note that never once in the entire narrative do we find Esau portrayed as devious or deceptive. That is Jacob's fatal flaw. Esau is not a total villain, and Jacob is not a pure hero. They are human beings with all their limitations and imperfections.

The Dream at Bethel

Jacob must have left home with a mixture of fear, defeat, depression, and, hopefully, guilt. The attempt to get the blessing had been a disaster. He must have wondered if even worse things might be in store for him. Had he ruined his life forever?

As he journeyed toward Haran he spent the nights out in the open, using a stone for a headrest. Isaac had given his son a parting blessing, the blessing of Abraham (verses 3, 4). The biblical writer now parallels the story of Abraham's blessing in Genesis 15. Abraham received a confirmation of the promises of the blessing in a vision (Gen. 15:1). God now gave Jacob a dream (Gen. 28:12). In it a ladder extended between heaven and earth (verse 12). Angels filed up and down it. The imagery in his dream would have been a familiar one in Jacob's world. The Akkadian counterpart to the Hebrew word translated "ladder" or "stairway" described the ramp the messengers of the gods used when traveling back and forth between this realm and that of the gods. The Babylonians built ziggurats to represent this divine stairway. Their gods would descend them to their temples on earth. Interestingly, though, the dream does not depict God traveling down the stairway to Jacob. Instead, the patriarch's God stands beside him (verse 13).

As He did with Abraham, the Lord promised that Canaan would belong to Jacob's children. But more important, He declared that He would bless all the people on earth through Jacob (verses 13, 14). The blessing was not limited just to his offspring. And as for Jacob himself, God would not abandon him (verse 15). The ancients normally considered a god to be tied to a particular geographical location. But Jacob's God would accompany him wherever he went.

The dream astonished Jacob. When he awoke, he exclaimed, "Surely the Lord is in this place—and I did not know it!" (verse 16). Overawed by a sense of the divine power and presence, he had no choice but to proclaim, "This is none other than the house of God, and this is the gate of heaven" (verse 17). Heaven and earth were in intimate contact, not through a temple, as the pagans believed, but through the actual presence of God Himself.

The next day, in a custom widespread in the ancient world, Jacob set up standing stones to memorialize his encounter with God. He called the place Bethel, "the house of God," and promised that if the Lord would continue with him, protecting him and providing life's necessities and bringing him back to Isaac's household, Jacob would worship Him as his God and would give Him a tenth of all that he received. Probably Jacob would have given his tithe in the form of sacrifices at Bethel.

The almost-600-mile trip to Haran would have taken more than a month. Most likely he would have joined a caravan for protection. Arriving in Mesopotamia, he encountered three flocks of sheep gathered around a well.[17] The shepherds were waiting for the removal of the covering stone. The stone protected the well from contamination and also discouraged unauthorized people from using the scarce water. Some commentators see the stone as so heavy that it required more than one person to lift. Others suggest that the shepherds of the various flocks did not trust each other and would not begin watering the animals until everyone had gathered. Then they could keep an eye on each other so that no one used more water than they should.

When Jacob learned that the shepherds were from Haran, he asked about Laban. They told him that all was well (literally, "peace") with Jacob's uncle and that his daughter Rachel approached at that very moment (Gen. 29:4-6). Seeing the girl, Jacob rolled the stone off the well all by himself, kissed her (a traditional act of greeting), and announced who he was. She hurried to notify her father about the visitor (verses 9-12). Because Jacob was kin and family ties were strong in the ancient world, Laban immediately brought him home.

The ancient world offered hospitality to visitors—but not on an unending basis. Apparently Jacob helped out with the household duties, and Laban began to see ways of profiting from the situation. He asked what kind of wages Jacob would accept to keep working for him (verse 15). Laban probably already had an idea what his nephew would be interested in. Perhaps Jacob had already told him the purpose of his mission to Haran— to find a wife. The narrator now mentions both of Laban's daughters.

The biblical author described Rachel as active (she sees, runs, and speaks) while portraying Leah as more passive. The narrative presents Rachel as beautiful and mentions Leah only as being older and as having eyes that the writer refers to by an ambiguous phrase variously translated as "there was no sparkle in Leah's eyes" or as "her eyes were lovely."[18] The reference to Leah's eyes may also subtly allude to Jacob's deception of his father because of Isaac's weak eyes.

By now Jacob had fallen in love with Rachel. Labor was an acceptable alternative for material goods as payment for the bride price. Jacob offered to work seven years for Rachel (verse 18), a rather high bride price. The seven years passed, and Jacob asked for his wife. Laban held a feast to celebrate the marriage. The Hebrew word for "feast" means drinking party, which may explain how Jacob did not realize that his father-in-law had switched Leah for Rachel. After Jacob woke up the next morning and discovered that he was now married to Leah, he demanded of Laban, "What is this you have done to me?" (verse 25). It recalls to the reader's mind "the same question addressed to his forebears

Abraham (Gen. 20:9) and Isaac (Gen. 26:10) when their deceptions involving their wives are uncovered."[19] The pattern of deception modeled by previous generations now repeats itself again—but with a twist. Jacob the trickster has himself been tricked.

Explaining that it was not the custom of his country to marry off a younger daughter before the older, Laban suggested that Jacob could have Rachel for another seven years of service. But first his son-in-law must complete the week of marriage celebration with Leah as sole wife.

Besides employing the substitution as a way of hanging on to Jacob's services, still other reasons motivated Laban to marry off Leah first. Even today it is the custom in the Middle East to make sure that the oldest daughter gets married first. "This prevents a younger sibling from shaming a sister who may not be as beautiful and also prevents the financial drain on the family caused by spinsters. Females were used, through marriage contracts, to obtain wealth and prestige for the family. If an older sister was bypassed and then never married, her family would be left with the responsibility to support her."[20]

Jacob now had two wives. Unfortunately he loved Rachel more than Leah. That fact would haunt all of them the rest of their lives and into the next generation.

---

[1] The whole Jacob story, beginning with Ishmael, the unchosen son, and ending with Esau, another unchosen son (Gen. 25:12-36:43), forms a complete chiastic structure with Jacob's return to Canaan after Joseph's birth as its center or focus.

[2] *Dictionary of Biblical Imagery,* ed. Leland Ryken, James C. Wilhoit, and Tremper Longman III (Downers Grove, Ill.: InterVarsity Press, 1998), p. 289. The firstborn was not necessarily the first child to enter a family. It involved honor more than chronology. The firstborn was dedicated to God (see D. I. Block, "Marriage and Family in Ancient Israel," pp. 82-84).

[3] Kenneth E. Bailey regards Jesus' parable of the prodigal son as His adaptation of the narrative of Jacob in Genesis 27:1-36:8. Bailey finds 51 points of parallel and/or counterbalance between the two stories. See Kenneth E. Bailey, *Jacob and the Prodigal: How Jesus Retold Israel's Story* (Downers Grove, Ill.: InterVarsity Press, 2003).

[4] Esau employs a verb meaning to stuff an animal with food.

[5] D. Kidner, *Genesis,* p. 152.

[6] J. H. Hellerman, *The Ancient Church as Family,* pp. 35-51. Unlike the modern obsession with marital strife and breakup, Scripture almost never dwells on marital problems. But it has endless accounts of sibling discord. Besides Jacob and Esau and the brothers of Joseph, the Bible tells of Aaron and Miriam's conflict with Moses and the turmoil among David's sons. The classic biblical account of sibling struggle is that of Cain and Abel. Both Scripture (John 3:12; Jude 11) and other ancient writers used it to symbolize ultimate wickedness (*ibid.,* pp. 40-43). For more background on understanding ancient family structure, see

Block, pp. 55-143; Victor H. Matthews, "Family Relationships," in *Dictionary of the Old Testament: Pentateuch,* ed. T. Desmond Alexander and David W. Baker (Downers Grove, Ill.: InterVarsity Press, 2003), pp. 291-299; Victor H. Matthews, "Israelite Society," in *Dictionary of the Old Testament: Historical Books,* ed. Bill T. Arnold and H.G.M. Williamson (Downers Grove, Ill.: InterVarsity Press, 2005), pp. 520-530; C. Meyers, "The Family in Early Israel," pp. 1-47; R. W. Younker, "Social Structure," in *Dictionary of the Old Testament: Pentateuch,* pp. 783-787.

[7] *New Bible Commentary: 21st Century Edition,* ed. D. A. Carson et al. (Leicester, Eng.: InterVarsity Press, 1994), p. 79.

[8] Hellerman, pp. 34, 35.

[9] *Dictionary of Biblical Imagery,* p. 98.

[10] *Ibid.,* pp. 894, 895.

[11] The verb "cried out" Scripture elsewhere uses in such laments as Psalm 77:1; 88:1; and 107:6, 28.

[12] J. L. Crenshaw, *Samuel,* p. 28.

[13] W. Brueggemann, *Genesis,* p. 285.

[14] *Ibid.*

[15] The biblical author has created another ring structure in the story of Isaac blessing his twin sons, one again displaying the literary artistry of biblical narrative:

> A   Isaac sends out Esau
> B   Rebekah instructs and disguises Jacob
> C   Jacob receives blessing from his father
> C   Esau receives his blessing
> B'   Rebekah makes marriage plans for Jacob
> A'   Isaac sends Jacob to Haran

Older scholars used to claim that the Bible was a rambling collection of material thrown together like a scissors-and-paste job. But today modern scholars recognize that it was carefully and intricately crafted.

[16] Brueggemann, p. 285.

[17] The encounter of a potential bride at a well forms a type scene in Scripture. In the Old Testament the reader first meets the wives of Isaac, Jacob, and Moses at a well. A possible New Testament counterpart to this type scene is the Samaritan woman at the well (John 4), though John gives it a different twist.

[18] G. Hens-Piazza, *Nameless, Blameless, and Without Shame,* pp. 108, 109.

[19] *HarperCollins Bible Commentary,* p. 101.

[20] J. H. Walton and V. H. Matthews, *The IVP Bible Background Commentary: Genesis to Deuteronomy,* p. 61.

11

Transformation

Genesis 29:31-36:43

The struggle between younger and older sisters has echoes of that between the older and younger brothers, Esau and Jacob. Their competition in giving birth was a desperate battle for identity and self-worth (Gen. 29:31-30:24). Again, as we have seen before in Genesis, they defined themselves solely by motherhood and the favor of their husband.[1] And in the process they were violating the relationship the Mediterranean world expected siblings to demonstrate.

Rachel's frustration at remaining childless intensified until she demanded of her husband, "Give me children, or I shall die!" (Gen. 30:1). Her statement was startling in a culture that blamed childlessness either on the woman or on God because He had prevented conception. Jacob angrily retorted, "Am I in the place of God, who has withheld from you the fruit of the womb?" (verse 2). She then resorted to a version of Sarah's scheme to get children. Jacob would father children by her maid, Bilhah (verses 3-8).

As we have seen, the household of Jacob has been a highly dysfunctional one. The way the members of a dysfunctional family are abused often becomes the pattern for how they will in turn abuse others. Laban had used his daughters as objects to manipulate Jacob to keep him in his service. Now Rachel and Leah employed their own servants to get what they wanted from their husband. Abuse spread through the extended family.

Bilhah was Rachel's slave—her property—and subject to her owner's authority. Rachel had the legal right in her culture to give the woman to

Jacob to bear children for her. But when Bilhah had sexual intercourse with Jacob, she became his wife (Gen. 30:4), though of a lesser status than either Rachel or Leah. Leah soon followed her sister's example (verses 9-13), and the same situation applied with Zilpah (verse 9). Both were now concubines—legal wives but with more limited rights. The two slave women, though, were still the property of their mistresses and could be disciplined. But once Bilhah and Zilpah had children by Jacob, their owners could no longer sell them.[2] While tolerated by contemporary culture, the situation was extremely unhealthy emotionally, especially in such a dysfunctional family as Jacob's.

One day Leah's son Reuben discovered some mandrake plants. They are stemless perennial roots that grow in stony ground. Perhaps because of its humanlike shape, the ancients used it in fertility rites and as an aphrodisiac. Since it is not common in Mesopotamia, Leah would have considered finding the plant a special stroke of luck. Later the two sisters would complain about their father selling them (Gen. 31:15). But now they bought and sold their own husband to father more children (verses 14-21). Although the wives might turn to mandrake plants to secure children, the narrator keeps reminding the reader that all the children ultimately came at God's intervention (Gen. 29:31, 33; 30:6, 17, 18, 20, 22, 23).

Rachel went childless for a long time, but eventually she had a son (Gen. 30:22, 23). The birth of Joseph triggered in Jacob a desire to return to Canaan (verses 25, 26), possibly because he had seen the fulfillment of the divine promise of children and protection. Additionally, patriarchal custom expected sons to live in the households of their fathers—not with the wife's family, as Jacob was now doing.[3] But Laban was not about to let his son-in-law leave. Jacob was too valuable. He told Jacob to name his wages (verse 28). Jacob acknowledged that he had been a source of blessing to Laban, but he wanted to concentrate on providing for his own household (verses 29, 30). Apparently law or custom forbade Jacob from leaving with his family and property without his father-in-law's permission (see Gen. 31:43). Eventually the two men worked out an agreement. It centered on the fact that most sheep were white and goats were black. Dark-colored lambs and variegated sheep and goats usually comprised only a small part of a typical herd. Because of that fact, Laban figured that he would not have to give up much to Jacob. (Shepherds also received part of the wool and milk products of the herd.)

Trickster that he was, Jacob came up with a scheme to get the flocks to breed to his advantage (Gen. 30:37-42). It seemed to work, and he prospered, growing richer and richer (verse 43). Later God would send him a dream that revealed that the solid-color animals actually carried the recessive genetic trait of multicolored offspring (Gen. 31:10-12). The Lord could not let him think that he was succeeding through his own efforts.

As Jacob became wealthier (apparently at the expense of Laban), Laban's sons began to complain (verse 1). Laban also grew increasingly hostile (verse 2). In a divine command that had echoes of His call to Abraham (Gen. 12:1-3), God told Jacob that it was time to return home (Gen. 31:3).[4] But the patriarch had to convince his wives to leave with him. After reminding them that their father had cheated him and repeatedly changed his wages (verses 6, 7), Jacob explained that God had manifested Himself to him in a dream. Declaring that He was the God of Bethel and that Jacob had made a vow to Him there, the Lord had said that Jacob must leave Mesopotamia immediately (verse 13). By referring to Himself as the God of Bethel, the Lord alluded to the vow that Jacob had made there (Gen. 28:20-22).

The wives were now willing to leave. They saw nothing worth staying in Haran for. "He has sold us, and he has been using up the money given for us" (Gen. 31:15). Verse 15 is the only biblical instance of the idea of selling a woman to another man to be his wife.[5] The fact that Laban's daughters were angry with their father implied that he did violate normal custom.[6] Walton and Matthews suggest that they might have been upset because he had not set aside the value of Jacob's labor (his way of paying the bride price) and as a result they would have no economic protection should their husband die. Thus there was no point in staying in Laban's household, so they might as well leave. It was as if their father had treated them as foreigners.[7] In a world that prized family relationships, he had behaved as if they were outsiders.

The Return to Canaan

Gathering his household and possessions, Jacob fled to Canaan. Foreshadowing Pharaoh in the Exodus, Laban pursued them. By the time he caught up, Jacob had reached the hill country of Gilead. God now intervened to protect Jacob, ordering the father-in-law not to harm him (verse 24). Despite the divine warning, Laban's encounter with Jacob was tense. At first he charged that Jacob had deceived him and kidnapped his daughters like prisoner of war (verse 26). Then he switched his approach, claiming that if Jacob had let him know that he was leaving, Laban would have held a celebration (verse 27). He accused his son-in-law of trying to deny him the opportunity to say goodbye to his daughters and grandchildren (verse 28). Next he admitted that he would have liked to punish them but that God had told him to do nothing (verse 29). Finally, he demanded to know why Jacob had stolen his *teraphim* (verse 30).[8]

Not knowing that Rachel had taken the *teraphim,* Jacob told Laban to search his camp. If anyone of his household had stolen them, he would punish the individual. Rachel had hidden them under a camel saddle that she sat on and prevented her father from examining by claiming that she was menstruating and thus she and the saddle were ceremonially unclean (verses 32-35). She had become as duplicitous as her father and husband.

The incident had echoes of Jacob's deception of Isaac. A youngest child had tricked a father to get something. The Hebrew verb "feel through" *(mashash)* in verses 34 and 37 is the same one the narrator employed to indicate the blind Isaac's "feeling" of Jacob (Gen. 27:22). Again the biblical author has shown his love for finding parallels and patterns.

Exploding from pent-up frustration and anger, Jacob demanded to know what he had done that Laban had to pursue him like a thief. He explained how he had taken nothing of Laban's during the entire 20 years that he had served him. If the Lord had not helped Jacob, his father-in-law would probably have sent him away with nothing. But "God saw my affliction and the labor of my hands, and rebuked you last night" in the dream Laban had had (Gen. 31:42).

Although still claiming the daughters and flocks as his, Laban offered to make a covenant with Jacob. In it he asked his son-in-law not to take any more wives. From ancient Nuzi documents it appears that such a stipulation seems intended to protect Leah's and Rachel's rights and marital status. But he had shown little concern for them up to this point. Jacob had two wives only because of Laban's scheming. Laban also wanted his son-in-law not to meddle in each other's territory. They solemnized the covenant by erecting a ceremonial pillar, offering a sacrifice, and sharing a meal. The meal sealed the covenant, and the sacrifice added to its solemnity. Jacob's conflict with Laban had received a resolution, but a greater one still faced the patriarch—that with Esau.

Esau's Reconciliation With Jacob

Jacob had dreamed of angels just before he left the Promised Land. Now he encountered another angel as he returned (Gen. 32). He also sent a message to his brother announcing his return. It let Esau know that his brother was not acting secretly (as he had so often in the past) and that he had not come to claim any inheritance rights. The messengers returned with the disturbing news that Esau was on his way to meet Jacob with 400 men, probably mercenaries and a large force for the time (verse 6). The patriarch turned to God, reminding Him that He Himself had told him to return to Canaan. Jacob asked the Lord to protect him from his brother and fulfill the divine promise of offspring as numerous as the sand of the seashore (verses 11, 12).

Choosing from his extensive herds and flocks, Jacob dispatched a large number of animals to his brother. "This gift would be sufficient for Esau to get a good start on a herding operation of his own or, alternatively, to reward any mercenaries in his employ who may have been anticipating booty."[9]

Jacob may have still been depending at least partially on his wits instead of relying fully on God. Besides being an attempt to appease his brother, the gifts could have had a more cynical motivation. The herds would have been a military liability for Esau. They would slow the brother down if Jacob had to flee. If nothing else, Esau would have had to leave some of his force with the herds to guard them. And by joining Esau's men, Jacob's servants could keep an eye on them and thus thwart an attack.

Perhaps the automatic desire to scheme his way out of trouble helps explain at least partially Jacob's encounter with the angel at the river Jabbok. The incident is as puzzling as God's command to Abraham to sacrifice his son. We find that both events test the faith of His chosen follower.

The angel at first seemed to threaten Jacob and his future just as the call to sacrifice appeared to doom the promised future of Abraham and his offspring. Jacob eventually prevailed in his struggle with the angel (and himself?). The divine being asked the patriarch to let Him go because it was almost dawn, perhaps reflecting the concept that in daylight Jacob would see him, and that no human being could see God and live (cf. verse 30; Ex. 33:20). When Jacob refused to release Him unless He blessed him, the angel changed Jacob's name, declaring, "You shall no longer be called Jacob, but Israel, for you have striven with God and with humans, and have prevailed" (Gen. 32:28). Jacob requested the angel's name, perhaps from the ancient Near Eastern belief that to know a god's secret name gave a person power over the deity. Naturally the angel rejected the attempt. He could not allow Jacob to play such a pagan game with Him.

Even a non–Israelite listening to the story of Jacob's encounter with the angel could have understood its significance. A Hittite ritual text tells of a struggle between a king and the goddess Khebat. The king refused to let the goddess go until he received a blessing.[10]

After his night of wrestling with the divine being, Jacob was finally able to assume his role as chosen leader of God's people. His new name may signify this fact. As we saw with Abraham, ancient suzerains sometimes changed a local ruler's name when they put them on the throne as vassals, so now God gave Jacob a new name. Changing a vassal's name demonstrated the overlord's power over him, and Jacob's new name showed God's power in his life.

Jacob named the place where he wrestled with the angel "Peniel," "the face of God," declaring, "For I have seen God face to face, and yet my life is preserved" (verse 30). The incident echoed his earlier encounter with God at Bethel (Gen. 28:19).

After the Jabbok experience Jacob began to take responsibility for what he had done to Esau, and he asked forgiveness for it.

Bible readers often regard Esau as the evil brother and Jacob as the good one. Yet the biblical depiction has been much more complex and has depicted the good and bad of both. Esau had every reason to seek revenge against Jacob when he learned of his brother's return. But instead he graciously welcomed his brother back. It seemed as if Esau had learned more easily to follow the Holy Spirit's leading than had his brother.

When the two brothers finally met face to face, Jacob bowed seven times to Esau, perhaps signifying that he now considered himself a vassal to his brother (Gen. 33:3).[11] It was a reversal of his father's prophecy in Genesis 27:29 and symbolically returned the blessing to Esau. Jacob continually referred to Esau as "my lord," stressing his submission to his older brother. The sibling who had stolen the primacy of the birthright now acknowledged the authority of the one he had illicitly seized it from.

Esau seemed more reconciled to Jacob than Jacob did to his twin. The older brother accepted Jacob's gift, thus sealing the reconciliation.[12] It was a return of the stolen birthright and blessing. When Esau offered to accompany Jacob along his journey, the brother politely declined (verses 12, 13). After urging Esau to go on ahead because his household and flocks would not be able to keep up with the older brother, Jacob promised to "come to my lord in Seir" (verse 14), Esau's home. But Jacob then immediately headed north to Succoth (verse 17). The biblical account never does mention him going to Seir. Did he revert to his old trickster mentality? Or was he just afraid of Esau, unable to trust him because he had been so long untrustworthy himself? Jacob also rejected Esau's offer of some of his retainers (verse 15). Clearly he remained suspicious of Esau even though his brother made no hostile moves.

Arriving at Shechem, Jacob bought some property. Like his grandfather Abraham, Jacob, the heir of the Promised Land, had to purchase a piece of it, again probably as a burial site as well as a place to live.

The Slaughter at Shechem

One day Jacob's daughter, Dinah, visited the local women—to tragic results. When Shechem, the son of Hamor the Hivite, the local ruler, saw her, he became infatuated with the girl. But he chose a brutal way of making her his wife—he raped her (Gen. 34:1, 2). People of the ancient Near East occasionally used rape as a means to force a marriage contract. Sexual intercourse was one way to formalize a marriage, but various ancient laws sought to restrict its violent misuse. Both Scripture (Ex. 22:16, 17; Deut. 22:28, 29) and Assyrian and Hittite regulations attempted to control the practice, often demanding that the man pay an extremely high bride price or forbidding the possibility of divorce. Forced marriage to someone who raped a woman shocks the modern Western sensibility, but "as a raped woman, she would no longer be eligible for marriage to another man, and hence marriage to her rapist gives her a socially sanctioned place in society."[13]

Shechem apparently did love the girl and attempted to woo her (Gen. 34:3). Furthermore, he asked his father to negotiate with Jacob to formalize the relationship further (verses 3, 4). Jacob did not initially respond either to the outrage (he "held his peace" [verse 5]) or to the father's request, but when his sons learned what had happened, they exploded (verse 7). In a part of the world that even today is obsessed with personal and family honor, they were perhaps more furious that Shechem had violated their family honor than that he had raped their sister. (No one in the discussion even mentioned her name or expressed any concern for her feelings. It was as if she had vanished from the story altogether.)

Hamor, even though he found himself in what was perhaps an impossible situation, tried to fulfill his son's request. He told Jacob and the brothers that "the heart of my son Shechem longs for your daughter; please give her to him in marriage" (verse 8). One of the main functions of marriage in the ancient world was the financial element. Marriage was the pooling of the resources of two families, and Hamor appealed to the economic advantages of the union. He urged Jacob and his sons and their clan to intermarry with the people of the city of Shechem. Such marriages would foster trade between the local people and Jacob's large family. It would also allow Jacob to purchase and own land (verse 10), instead of having to wait for God to give it to him.

The son also pleaded for Dinah's family to allow the marriage to continue. His participation was unusual because the father normally did the negotiation of the bride price for his children's marriages. Shechem would pay any price Dinah's family demanded, no matter how high (verses 11, 12).[14] The girl had become an object to bargain over.

The brothers—not Jacob—had a suggestion. As they would do repeatedly, they were usurping Jacob's rightful role in marital arrangements. And lest his audience also be fooled by the brothers, the biblical narrator explicitly announced that they were speaking "deceitfully" (verse 13).

After stating that it would disgrace their family to offer their sister to someone who did not practice their custom of circumcision, they offered a proposal. If all the males among Hamor and Shechem's people would accept the rite of circumcision, Jacob's clan would be willing to intermarry with them. But it was a take-it-or-leave-it deal (verses 14-17).

Hamor's son was more than willing to accept the arrangement. "The proposed condition of settlement seems a proper one, even to Shechem. The solution offers benefits to both parties. On the one hand, it permits *cooperation* and intermarriage. On the other hand, it insists on the *religious peculiarity* of Israel which must be honored."[15]

Immediately father and son approached their community leaders at the gate and emphasized the economic and political advantages of the potential relationship with Jacob and his powerful clan. "Will not their livestock, their property, and all their animals be ours?" (verse 23). They persuaded the men of Shechem to undergo the rite of circumcision (verse 24).

Circumcision was the symbol of God's relationship with the lineage of Abraham. Abraham's descendants were to bless the nations. But Jacob's sons turned the sign of the covenant into a means to get revenge on Shechem and his people. While the men were still crippled by the pain of the rite, Simeon and Levi slaughtered the males. Jacob's sons also seized their property, wives, and children (verses 25-29). The women and children would become slaves. Not only were the sons after revenge; their taking the flocks and other property revealed that they had been coveting the wealth of the local inhabitants.

The violent act of revenge shocked Jacob—but in a rather self-centered way. "You have brought trouble on me by making me odious to the inhabitants of the land," he told them in horror. If the local people should unite and attack, "I shall be destroyed, both I and my household" (verse 30). But his sons were unfazed. "Should our sister be treated like a whore?" (verse 31). Rape was not prostitution. All they could think of was revenging family honor, an obsession that continues even today in many cultures and frequently leads to death and a cycle of more revenge. Even worse—if possible—the sons were totally blind to the consequences of what they had done.

The people of the surrounding region could hardly ignore the actions of Jacob's sons. Who knew when these aliens might go berserk again? The safest course would be to destroy them before it happened. It would be only a matter of time before the Canaanites and others wiped out Jacob's family, just as his sons had done to the people of Shechem.

God recognized the precarious situation Jacob now found himself in, and directed him to move to Bethel and erect an altar there (Gen. 35:1). Bethel was where God had revealed Himself when the patriarch had fled the Promised Land because of his fear of Esau. Jacob needed that divine assurance of God's presence once again. At Bethel the patriarch instructed his household to purify the defilement they had brought upon themselves through the slaughter of the men of Shechem. Genesis 34 had frequently used the word "defile" (Gen. 34:5, 13, 27). Now Genesis 35:2 speaks of "purify." By putting away the pagan images and burying the earrings, they dedicated themselves to God. "Israel engages in dramatic ritual activity as a mode of faithfulness."[16] And as the large household slowly journeyed to Bethel, the Lord caused the surrounding people to fear and not pursue them (verse 5). God also appeared once more to Jacob and reaffirmed the promises He had given to Abraham (verses 9-12).

Jacob had begun a transformation, signified by his new name, Israel, but what he had modeled to his family continued to do damage. Reuben shocked everyone and dishonored his father by having a sexual affair with Bilhah, Jacob's concubine. As we have noted before, concubines were legal wives, though of a lesser status and without dowries. Reuben's act would have been seen as incestuous (having sex with his father's wife) and an attempt to usurp Jacob's authority in the family. The latter practice would soon repeat itself.

At last Jacob returned to his father's household. Decades before, Isaac had used the possibility of his impending death as an excuse to give Esau the special blessing. Finally he did die, and the twin brothers united to bury and mourn him (verses 27-29). The last we see of the two brothers together is at their father's funeral. They were performing one of the most sacred duties of a family in the biblical world—burying its dead.[17] After burying Isaac, they divided their households and flocks peacefully and settled some distance from each other in echo of the separation of Abraham and Lot (Gen. 36:6-9). No stigma falls on Esau.[18] Genesis gives a lengthy genealogy of Esau,[19] showing his importance. As Abraham's two sons founded two nations (Gen. 21:13), so Isaac's sons would each be the progenitor of a nation.

"The free choice of Jacob by Yahweh (25:23) is sure and unchallenged in the narrative. But Esau is there, very much there."[20] Just because God elected Jacob did not mean that He had rejected Esau. When God changed Abram's name to Abraham, He told the patriarch that He would make "nations" of him (Gen. 17:6). Ishmael founded one nation and now Esau another. What could God have accomplished if the two brothers—especially Jacob—had chosen a different way of relating to each other?

---

[1] We see frequently this frantic desire for children by barren women elsewhere in the Old Testament as well as in extrabiblical documents (J. H. Hellerman, *The Ancient Church as Family,* pp. 33, 34).

[2] D. I. Block, "Marriage and Family in Ancient Israel," p. 78.

[3] Hellerman, p. 33.

[4] As pointed out in a previous note, the birth of Joseph and the decision to return to Canaan is the pivotal point of the literary structure of the Jacob story.

[5] Block, p. 63.

[6] For a refutation of the idea that the wife was just another of the man's possessions, see Block, pp. 61-69.

[7] J. H. Walton and V. H. Matthews, *The IVP Bible Background Commentary: Genesis-Deuteronomy,* pp. 62, 63.

[8] Scholars debate whether the *teraphim* are household gods or images of dead ancestors. Many commentators assume that whatever the identity of the objects, they had something to do with inheritance or fertility. Rachel took them perhaps as compensation for his defrauding her of her bride price.

[9] Walton and Matthews, p. 65.

[10] *Ibid.*

[11] Fourteenth-century B.C. Egyptian texts from El Armana tell of vassals bowing seven times to the pharaoh (Walton and Matthews, p. 66).

[12] D. Kidner, *Genesis,* p. 171.

[13] *The IVP Women's Bible Commentary,* ed. Catherine Clark Kroeger and Mary J. Evans (Downers Grove, Ill.: InterVarsity Press, 2002), p. 23.

[14] Perhaps the willingness to pay any bride price no matter how extravagant is an implicit acknowledgment of the fact that the son has dishonored Dinah *(ibid.).*

[15] W. Brueggemann, *Genesis,* p. 276.

[16] *Ibid.,* p. 281.

[17] Hellerman, pp. 50, 51, 72, 73.

[18] Brueggemann, p. 285.

[19] The list of Esau's descendants parallels the genealogical list of Genesis 25. Both lists show that God cares for even those not in the direct line of the chosen.

[20] Bruggemann, p. 286.

12

A Family Destroying Itself

Genesis 37:1-41:40

Jacob had always loved Rachel more than Leah, and this love continued to manifest itself even after her death. He displayed obvious favoritism toward Rachel's children, Joseph and Benjamin. We first see
Joseph as a 17-year-old shepherd helping some of his half brothers, the sons
of Bilhah and Zilpah. Apparently they did something that disturbed Joseph,
and he reported it to his father (Gen. 37:2). The story does not elaborate
on what they did. The author is interested only in Joseph's behavior.
Although in his time society would have considered Joseph a fully mature
adult, the scriptural account reports him as acting more like a tattling child.
Siblings were to protect, not harm, each other. The biblical world was obsessed with honor and shame.[1] Joseph's report shamed the brothers in their
father's eyes. In addition, Jacob's wives had fought each other through
their servants. Now Joseph perpetuated that discord by getting the sons of
the handmaidens into trouble. The favored son drove still another wedge
between the members of his family.

Jacob doted on Joseph because "he was the son of his old age" (verse
3). To show his regard for Joseph, the father had "a long robe with sleeves"
made for him. Traditional translations have rendered it as a coat of many
colors. Walton and Matthews observe that while the coat may have been
colorful, it was the material, fine weave, and length that made it valuable.
We may get a hint of what the garment looked like from depictions of
well-dressed Canaanites in Egyptian tomb paintings. They wore long-
sleeved embroidered costumes with a fringed scarf extending diagonally

from waist to knee.[2] Such garments would have taken a long time to weave and would thus have been extremely valuable. If, as is most probable, Jacob's own weavers (generally the women of a household) manufactured it, the rest of the family would have known of its existence and potential recipient long before they finished it. The garment would have aroused hostility from the very beginning. The same term in 2 Samuel 13:18 refers to clothing worn by royalty. Jacob clearly intended his gift to represent authority as well as favor. Yet Joseph was the next-to-youngest son in a culture that ranked the role and honor of sons by their birth order. Jacob, who had wanted the honor of firstborn, now violated the principle of Deuteronomy 21:15-17 by focusing his affection on Joseph, the next to last of all of his sons.

The robe not only indicated that Jacob favored Joseph over his other sons; it slapped them in the face by ignoring all they understood about their place in the family. The father had earlier turned his family upside down by trying through his own efforts to reverse birth order and birthright. Now he did it again with his own sons. Jacob was still destroying family relationships. The Bible does not depict the brothers only as villains or stereotypes of evil. As much victim as Joseph soon would be, they recognized arbitrary love when they saw it, and it understandably evoked their hatred.[3] Since they could not do anything about their father, they vented their anger on the more loved son. The brothers found themselves caught between Joseph and Jacob. Their frustration eventually left them unable even to carry on a peaceful conversation with Joseph (Gen. 37:4).

The opening verses of the Joseph story depict a family destroying itself. The author reinforced this fact by placing the brothers' hatred of Joseph "against a background of relational and familial language: 'son(s)' occurs five times, 'father' four times, and 'brothers' three times."[4] Furthermore, none of them were free from guilt. Jacob flaunted his favoritism, Joseph stirred up family strife by reporting on his brothers, and the brothers gave in to their hatred.[5]

Joseph's Dreams

Then Joseph further antagonized them by describing two dreams he had had. In the first he and his brothers were binding sheaves of grain in the field. The sheaves were bundles of stalks quickly tied together and laid on the ground. But his bundle stood up, and those prepared by the other brothers gathered around it and bowed down (verses 5-7). The listening brothers instantly recognized the dream's implication. Such dreams of a rise in power were a standard motif in the ancient Near East. For example, hundreds of years earlier Sargon, king of Akkad, had had such a dream of his eventual assumption of rulership.[6] In Egypt one pharaoh claimed to have had a dream in which the Sphinx told him that he would unexpectedly become king. Joseph's brothers could in no way misinterpret what he was saying. Their younger brother was announcing that he would have authority over them. Again he was violating the ancient cultural understanding that sons had priority by order of birth.

To compound his audacity and insult, Joseph related a second dream,[7] in which the sun, moon, and 11 stars bowed down to him (verse 9). Jacob reacted to it in anger. "What kind of dream is this that you have had?" he demanded. "Shall we indeed come, I and your mother[8] and your brothers, and bow to the ground because of you?" (verse 10). His brothers' jealousy only worsened.

Joseph's dreams foreshadowed the rest of his life, providing a motivation and explanation of what would happen to him.[9] God gave them to him, but each member of the family, including Joseph himself, chose how they would respond to them. Joseph was too immature and self-centered to realize what presenting the dreams would do to his family. The brothers responded as if the dreams were fuel tossed into the furnace of their hatred and rage. They did not even bother to speak to him. Only the father seemed to be open to the dreams, as he "kept the matter in mind" (verse 11). Perhaps Jacob had learned "by now, as his sons had not, to allow for God's hand in affairs, and for His right of choice among men."[10] After all, he had seen what could result when one tried to take charge of God's plans.

Would God have worked the dreams out in ways other than He did if Joseph and the others had made different choices? We can never know for sure, but John Sanders points out that at least one aspect of the dream was never fulfilled. The detail about Joseph's father and "mother" was conditional, because it never happened.[11] Both Rachel (Gen. 35:16-20) and Leah (Gen. 49:31) died in Canaan, and the biblical account never mentions Jacob bowing to Joseph. It is possible that Joseph's family could have avoided much pain and tragedy in the succeeding years by following different courses. At least, all bore guilt and responsibility for how they related to one another.

In many ways Joseph lived a moral life as a young person. He could not have resisted the temptations of Egypt otherwise. But one can be highly moral and yet immature at the same time. Joseph had much to learn. Through the dreams God indicated that He had great plans for him.

But the young man could not fulfill them until he had grown and matured in character.

Confrontation at Dothan

The brothers took the family flocks toward the north, to Shechem (Gen. 37:12). Jacob sent Joseph to "see if it is well" with them (verse 14).[12] The Hebrew word translated "well" here is *shalom,* "peace." But Joseph would find no peace when he met his brothers. Reaching Shechem, he discovered them gone (verses 14-17). A man encountered him wandering in the empty fields. Joseph was lost in more ways than he realized. The stranger asked him whom he was looking for. The young man explained that he had come to see his brothers and inquired where they might be pasturing their flocks now (verse 16). The unnamed man replied that he heard them talking about going to Dothan (verse 17), thus helping Joseph find his way—a journey that would unexpectedly take him through Egypt. Could the stranger have been an agent of providence sent to guide the immature son on his way to the experiences that would lead him to maturity and greatness?

Much was going on in this seemingly simple incident that escapes the attention of the modern reader, because few of us live in a pastoral world. People in the biblical world would have quickly recognized something wrong. The brothers had no right to move the flocks.

Vegetation and water were (and are) scarce in Palestine, and, as we observed with Abraham and Lot, herds could not remain long in any one place before they exhausted one or both. Usually as the wetter winter season turned into the dry summer, herders would first graze their flocks in harvested fields, then lead them both north and to higher elevations, where enough vegetation still remained. (The annual rainfall increases as one travels north.) Springs and wells would run dry, also forcing the herds to move on. But pastoralists could not graze their flocks just anywhere. Again we must remember that all the land suitable for pasture already belonged to someone. Farmers did not want flocks destroying their unharvested crops or depleting their water sources. Thus laws carefully stipulated and guarded grazing rights.[13] Besides, too many herds in one place for too long could strip the land bare, causing erosion. Tensions always existed between the landowners and wandering pastoralists such as Jacob and his family. (Some of the people of Canaan both raised crops and tended livestock part of the year. As we noted elsewhere, they would have had first rights on grazing land.) To complicate matters further, Jacob and his household were resident aliens in a land of limited and already strained resources. They were outsiders in a closely knit world. To survive, Jacob and his clan had to be willing to live by the rules set by the permanent inhabitants of the land.[14]

Sheepherders had to pay for the right to graze another person's land. It required careful and extensive negotiations, as we see in such passages as Genesis 21:22-33.[15] Pastoralists had to arrange for grazing rights before the start of the agricultural season in any one spot. Only the head of a household or his designated representative could make such a treaty. Herders could not move their flocks at will, especially on a whim.

Yet the brothers had done exactly that. Jacob had expected them to be at Shechem, because he had negotiated the treaty with the local landowners there. He knew nothing about current grazing rights anywhere else. When the brothers shifted the flocks to Dothan, they had usurped his cultural role as negotiator and treatymaker. Only he had the ultimate authority to shift the flocks, and only after he had established a treaty with the owners of the pasture site. Sons in the biblical world could not make such decisions on their own as long as their fathers were still alive or if the latter had not given them authority to negotiate for them. The fact that Joseph had to hunt for his brothers shows that neither he nor Jacob knew anything about their transferring to Dothan. Jacob had not given them permission to go anywhere else. The brothers had made the decision for themselves. In their culture they were acting as if their father were already dead. Perhaps their frustration and anger at how he treated them had destroyed their respect for him. More likely they were just behaving as their father had done all his life. Jacob had deceived his father—now his sons were deceiving him. And the pattern would continue.

When the brothers spotted Joseph approaching them, all the resentment at him and their father burst into the flames of murder. If they could kill the dreamer, it would also destroy the dreams. With Joseph dead they would never have to worry about bowing down to him (Gen. 37:18-21). He would stop running their lives, turning everything upside down. Could the final spark that ignited their rage have been the fear that Joseph would report to their father their decision to move the flocks? They had had enough shame.

Reuben, however, managed to talk them out of killing Joseph immediately. He suggested that they throw their brother into an empty cistern. The narrator steps out from the background and tells us what is in Reuben's mind: he wanted to rescue Joseph and restore him to their father (verse 22). Perhaps he hoped also to mend his relationship (damaged by his affair with Bilhah) with his father. Then the brothers sat down to eat (verse 25). Meals are supposed to be a time of family and social bonding. But this mealtime was only a prelude to a terrible shattering of family ties that would have to be reformed during other meals years later (Gen. 42; 43). They ate while Joseph huddled alone in the pit, not knowing that the same thing would repeat itself under very different circumstances. Joseph would then also be by himself as the brothers shared a meal together (Gen. 43:32). Noticing a spice caravan on its way to Egypt, Judah suggested that they sell Joseph to it as a slave (Gen. 37:25-28). Apparently Reuben had gone off on some errand.

When he returned and found Joseph gone, Reuben tore his clothing in the ancient biblical ritual of morning (verse 29), a foreshadowing of his father's grief (verse 34). Jacob had tricked his father with a goatskin. His sons would lie to him with the aid of the blood of another goat. Their father had honored Joseph with a special garment. Now they would dishonor him with that same piece of clothing. A gift of warped love had turned into a symbol of cruel hatred.

The anguished father ripped his robes and wrapped his body in sackcloth (verse 34). His sons and daughter sought to comfort him, but his grief was inconsolable (verse 35). What must the brothers have thought as they went through the motions of helping him with a grief that they had themselves caused?

Verses 18-33 form a unit that has the brothers suggesting to each other that they kill Joseph and tell their father that "a wild animal has devoured him" (verse 20), and ends with Jacob sobbing out, "A wild animal has devoured him" (verse 33). Again we find a ring or concentric pattern, and the author has placed his main point in the middle of the unit. Here it is Judah's proposal to sell Joseph (verses 26, 27). The brothers attempted to get rid of Joseph, but divine providence took over and planted in Judah's mind the idea that they dispose of the brother as a slave instead. The Ishmaelites would take Joseph to where God wanted him.

Judah and Tamar

The biblical writer unexpectedly interrupted his story of Joseph with that of one involving Judah. The brothers as a whole had sent Joseph away from the family into Egyptian slavery. Echoing Joseph's disappearance, Judah for some unknown reason left the rest of his brothers and settled near a man named Hirah the Adullamite (Gen. 38:1). There he married the unnamed and perhaps Canaanite daughter of a man called Shua. Soon Judah had three sons by her (verses 2-5). He married off the oldest one, Er, to Tamar, apparently also a Canaanite woman. But Er behaved wickedly, and "the Lord put him to death" (verse 7). Again the theme of family survival surfaces in the book of Genesis when Judah instructed the second son, Onan, to fulfill the levirate custom of fathering a child by his brother's widow to preserve that line of the family. Onan deliberately avoided getting her pregnant, and God caused his death (verses 8-10). Afraid that the same fate would strike the third son, Shelah, and end Judah's line as well, the patriarch sent Tamar back to her father with the excuse that she would have to wait until Shelah reached marriageable age (verse 11).

Not only did levirate marriage preserve the family line; it also protected the widow. Ancient society defined a woman's status by her relationships to males, either her husband or her sons. Tamar, as a childless widow, had no status or identity, nor did she have a male relative to support and protect her. By sending her back to her father, Judah rejected any responsibility for her, leaving Tamar in what would be in her culture a kind of legal, economic, and social limbo.

An unspecified period of time passed, and Tamar waited for her father-in-law to fulfill his responsibility of sending the third son to her. Reflecting the high mortality rate of ancient women, Judah's wife died (verse 12). Sheepshearing season commenced soon after Judah completed his formal period of mourning for his wife, and he and his friend Hirah set out for the camp of his shepherds at Timnah. By now Tamar had become frustrated by Judah's refusal to do anything about her situation. Hearing that he had left to supervise the sheepshearing, she came up with a plan to force his hand. She would trick him (Genesis is populated with tricksters) into meeting his cultural responsibility to her.

Sheepshearing was traditionally a time of feasting and celebration that could slide into sexual activity. She figured that Judah, now a widower, would become lonely, and she would take advantage of that fact. Removing her widow's garment, she veiled herself. Neither a married woman nor a widow wore veils at this time, but prostitutes would as an indication of their profession. (By New Testament times the custom had reversed itself, married women at least in Jerusalem and cities using the veil and prostitutes going about with uncovered heads.)

When Judah encountered her on the way to Timnah, he assumed she was a prostitute and negotiated with her, offering her a goat kid for her favors. She demanded a pledge and asked for his seal and personal walking staff (verses 13-18). He probably thought that she did not trust him to pay her afterward, but she wanted the two easily identified objects for another reason.

Since few could write their names, people used seals to authenticate a contract or other document. Artisans carved the seals with distinctive images that could be rolled across a clay tablet or pressed on wax or blobs of clay used to seal the cords tying a scroll. Wealthy individuals would have their seals made from precious or semiprecious stones. The seal's owner might wear it threaded on a leather cord suspended around the neck or wound around the arm. People would employ the seal for business transactions somewhat the way moderns would a credit card. Staffs might be distinctively carved. Friends, trading partners, and others would be able to recognize a specific person's staff and seal.

Tamar conceived as a result of the sexual encounter and retreated back into her role of anonymous widow. When Judah sent the agreed-upon payment by his friend Hirah, the woman was nowhere to be found. Judah figured that to search for her further might draw embarrassing attention, and decided to let the unknown prostitute keep the signet and staff (verse 20-23).

Three months later he learned that his daughter-in-law was pregnant. Without any kind of investigation or hearing, he unjustly declared her guilty and ordered her death by burning. As Judah's men led her away for execution, she showed them the personal seal and staff and told them, "It was the owner of these who made me pregnant." Then she added, "Take note, please, whose these are, the signet and the cord and the staff" (verse 25).

"Her statement and request are deferential in tone, as benefits her subordinate status. She does not confront or accuse Judah, yet the evidence speaks loud and clear. Judah acknowledges the items and his own guilt and holds up Tamar for honor."[16] Both Tamar and Judah used the same Hebrew word, nakar ("to recognize"), when she said, "Take note" (verse 25), and he "acknowledged" (verse 26) that the seal and staff were his. The word appeared twice in the previous chapter when the brothers said to Jacob, "See now whether it is your son's robe or not" (Gen. 37:32), and the biblical narrator stated that Jacob "recognized" it (verse 33). Chapter 38 has deliberate echoes of chapter 37. Perhaps the author wanted to show Tamar's cultural superiority to the brothers.

Her father-in-law's statement that "she is more in the right" (Gen. 38:26) sounds strange to the modern Western mind. Some English translations render it as "She is more righteous than I." The Old Testament concept of righteousness builds upon the twin concepts of right relationships and upholding rights and justice. "When . . . Judah says of Tamar, 'She is righteous, rather than I,' he has in view his contention with her, not a general assessment of her character. Her way of becoming pregnant, deceptive though it was, conformed to the norm for preserving the familial line of her deceased husband; she was pregnant by Judah himself. . . . Judah's behavior is called 'unjust' in that he had intercourse with Tamar incognito, supposing her to be a prostitute, and yet was prepared to execute judgment on his daughter-in-law for 'playing the whore.'"[17]

Tamar sought to fulfill her proper role in providing an heir for her dead husband. By refusing to give her his third and final son, he denied her justice. He robbed her of the economic protection that having a son would guarantee a woman in her culture, and in the course of events even threatened his own family line. She was more faithful to his family heritage than he had been. Although what she did may be questionable in modern eyes, she upheld her world's custom and tradition. Her twin sons gave Judah descendants (verses 26-30). Their birth echoes that of their grandfather, Jacob, and his brother, Esau (verses 28-30). And she would receive honor in the history of Israel (Ruth 4:12, 18; Matt. 1:3).

Genesis 38 also has parallels with the surrounding story of Joseph. In it "a kid again becomes part of the mix-up (38:17 and 20), clothes serve as a disguise, and denouement consists of a recognition that causes a great shock (vv. 24-26) sets [Judah] up for his major role as the brothers' spokesman in Genesis 44, and prepares us for Judah's crucial speech at the Egyptian court."[18] It also set up a contrast between Joseph's moral behavior and the lack of it on Judah's part. In Genesis 38 a foreign woman with higher moral values bested the immoral Judah. But in Genesis 39 an immoral foreign woman would try to triumph over the principled Joseph—only to fail.

Victor P. Hamilton observes that "chapter 38 is in microcosm what chapters 37 and 39-50 are in macrocosm. God works his plan even in unsavory circumstances. Joseph survives hostility and becomes the physical salvation of his family. Zerah and Perez, twins in the messianic line (Matt. 1:3), have their origin in an incestuous relationship between father-in-law and daughter-in-law."[19]

Joseph in Potiphar's House

In Egypt Joseph became the property of Potiphar, captain of the palace guard (Gen. 39:1). Again the biblical author makes his own voice heard, telling the reader that God was with the young man (verse 2),[20] a fact that the Egyptian official also recognized (verse 3). Joseph, after going "down" to Egypt, quickly "rises" in Potiphar's service (verses 2-6). But he was not the only one to notice Joseph's success. The slave became the target of his master's wife, and she attempted to seduce him (verse 7).[21] He rebuffed her advances (verses 8-10).

Egypt was rather casual about sexual relationships except for adultery with another man's wife. That Egyptians took quite seriously,[22] especially since it shamed the husband of the adulterous woman. And that was guaranteed to make the culprit the target of his wrath. Yet Joseph did not defend his refusal to commit adultery with Potiphar's wife on the grounds that it would dishonor the husband. Rather he saw it as dishonoring his God.

Finally she abandoned words and suggestions and resorted to action. When they were alone in the house one day, she brazenly grabbed his clothing and demanded, "Lie with me!" (verse 12). Although she hung on to his garment, he pulled himself free and fled naked outside (verse 12). (Jacob's family constantly seem to be getting into trouble because of something they wear.)[23]

Tremper Longman III points out that the Joseph fulfilled the description of the ideal man of Proverbs 5-7,[24] but, as so often happens in real life, it did not protect him from disaster.

Sermons and devotional writings have turned Potiphar's wife into little more than a symbol of pure evil and sexual lust, and Joseph into a stereotyped example of unsullied virtue, But both were real, complex beings. Life is never so simplistic, so black and white. Could there have been more than just sexual desire behind her attempted seduction? What does the incident have to say to those of us who have to make decisions in an often ambiguous world? And could those additional issues teach us something about what God hoped Joseph would learn from being allowed to go through such an experience?

The ancient world, including Egypt, divided reality into two spheres: home, and the world beyond it. In many ways they were two parallel societies. Men were responsible for the one outside the home, and women took care of the social world inside it. We must not view these dual worlds through the imaginary stereotypes of 1950s American television programs in which the wife stayed home to cook, clean, and raise children while the husband went off to the office or factory to earn a living for the whole family. Rather, the ancient household was for all practical purposes a complete economy in itself, requiring complex management and technical skills to operate it.

Families in the biblical world did not go out and buy food, clothing, or whatever they needed. Instead, especially in the rural areas, they personally had to raise or make everything. And women did almost all of this work. "Considerable expertise—planning, skill, experience, and technological knowledge—was necessary for the performance of a woman's tasks, many of which involved precise chemical and physical processes."[25] Carol Meyers observes that around the home and farm "female tasks required a higher degree of expertise, judgment, and skill than did male tasks."[26] It takes as much executive skill and insight to manage a household as it does a business or government.

Today modern Western society sees many advantages for both genders participating in each sphere of life, but the ancient world preferred to keep them separate, and Egypt was no exception.[27] Joyce Tyldesley states that in ancient Egypt "the married woman's most coveted title of Mistress of the House was a constant reminder of her principal wifely duty: to ensure the smooth day-to-day running of her husband's home. It seems very unlikely that either sex would ever have dreamed of questioning the inevitability of this division of labor. Males and females were understood by all to be different types of people destined to live very different lives, and an upsetting of this natural order would clearly have been wrong."[28]

The wife's rightful domain was the home. A woman on the social level of Potiphar's wife would have had charge of numerous servants and the extensive production done in the household. Each household manufactured most of the goods (textiles, pottery, and much of the food) that it needed to survive. Wealthier Egyptian households were equivalent to small villages.

When Potiphar put Joseph in charge of his household, he placed his slave in a woman's role. Usually we think of Joseph's assignment from the perspective of a modern business manager. But as we have seen, the household was the wife's domain and responsibility. While the husband was the theoretical head of the household, the wife or dominant woman (such as a mother-in-law or sister-in-law) held the actual power. Joseph specifically stated to Potiphar's wife that his master "is not greater in this house than I am" (Gen. 39:9). Potiphar and Joseph were equals in the household. Theoretically the wife had two men over her. The difference between them was that she was Potiphar's wife, not his, and he competed with her for authority in her own household. From any perspective Joseph had a most unusual role in Egyptian society.

Why would Potiphar go against cultural custom? Perhaps we can suggest two reasons—one on the human level and the other on the divine. The latter Joseph alluded to when he told his brothers that not they but God had sent him to Egypt (Gen. 45:8).

As for the human motivation on Potiphar's part, we first need to consider why he kept Joseph in prison after the wife accused the slave of attempted rape. Until fairly recently in human history prisons were just holding places until the convicted criminal was executed, forced to pay a fine, sold into slavery, or punished in some other way. Prison was not a long-term thing. Yet Potiphar confined Joseph there for a number of years. It was as if the Egyptian official did not know what to do with his Hebrew slave.

Could he in the first place have put Joseph in charge of his household—traditionally a woman's role—because of some problem between him and his wife? We cannot know. But whatever the reason, when he replaced her with Joseph, it shamed her in the eyes of her world. Did she then, as Joseph's brothers had earlier when they found themselves caught between Joseph and their father, seek revenge? If so, she would employ any means available to strike back at her husband, and what better way than seducing the man who had replaced her? Yes, Joseph was good-looking, but was the really irresistible attraction the fact that to do so would mock and dishonor the husband who had removed her from her rightful place? She could enjoy the slave's physical charms and also know that she had made a fool of the man who had usurped her rightful role in life. And did Potiphar hesitate to execute Joseph for rape or refrain from selling him elsewhere because he sensed the young man's innocence? Did he guess that his wife had initiated the encounter because of their strained relationship? Had his plan to oust his wife from her cultural role backfired and did he now feel guilty because of the harm it brought Joseph? We can only speculate. If the wife did lure Joseph into a trap, it does not excuse what she did, but it helps us to understand better why she behaved as she did.

If Joseph did find himself caught between Potiphar and his wife, it echoes the experience of all God's people. They may feel themselves the helpless pawns of forces out of their control. Perhaps people even have what appear to be understandable motives for what they do wrong. But that does not lessen the responsibility of God's people to do right. Perhaps Potiphar unfairly pushed his wife out of her defining role in life. But that did not give Joseph any excuse to commit adultery with her. No matter how overwhelming the pressures against us may appear, we still have control over how we react.

In addition, we find a great irony in Joseph's experience in the household of Potiphar. From a divine perspective, it was as if God knew that by fulfilling a woman's duties Joseph would become a better man. His dreams had foretold that someday people would bow down to him. To become a good ruler he must first become a faithful servant. Men might get away with being incompetent administrators, but a family starved if a woman fell down on her job. Women took care of the household, the basic unit of ancient culture. What better training could Joseph get? As he had prospered in Potiphar's household, God was preparing him for service in Pharaoh's household and the nation of Egypt.

Potiphar put Joseph in prison, but God was protecting the Hebrew slave. Divine providence usually works through human motivation and action. Clearly Potiphar did not fully believe his wife, for whatever reason. Walton and Matthews suggest that Potiphar's choice of prison did indeed indicate that he understood the nature of the encounter between his servant and his wife. "Rather than being executed for rape . . . , Joseph was put into a royal prison holding political prisoners. This may have been a bit more comfortable (as prisons go), but more importantly it will put him into contact with members of Pharaoh's court (Gen. 40:1-23)."[29] It is almost as if Pharaoh's official had to do something to protect his honor, but he wanted the punishment as mild as possible.

God continued to watch over Joseph. "He gave him favor in the sight of the chief jailer" (Gen. 39:21). As he had in Potiphar's house, even in prison Joseph became in charge of everything, so that "the chief jailer paid no heed to anything that was in Joseph's care, because the Lord was with him; and whatever he did, the Lord made it prosper" (verse 23; cf. verses 2-6). Earlier Joseph had had a double set of dreams. Now we encounter the second pair of three sets of paired dreams. The king had placed his royal cupbearer and baker in the prison until he could decide their fate (Gen. 40:1-3). A cupbearer's main role was to test the king's food and drink and protect him from poisoning. He would thus have been a highly trusted individual. Potiphar put both him and the baker in Joseph's care (verse 4). Both soon had disturbing dreams (verse 5).

When Joseph observed that they seemed troubled, he asked what was bothering them. They explained that they had had dreams whose sense eluded them. Even worse, they had no one to interpret the dreams.[30] Joseph encouraged them to describe the dreams to him. His God would understand their meaning (verses 5-8). After the cupbearer related his dream (verses 9-11), Joseph stated that the official would regain his position (verses 12, 13), and requested that the Egyptian mention him to Pharaoh and get him out of prison. Joseph had been kidnapped from his home country[31] and had done nothing to deserve his present situation (verses 14, 15).

Unfortunately, the baker's dream did not lead to such a happy resolution. Pharaoh had him executed. Joseph's interpretations came to pass, but apparently for naught. The cupbearer forgot about him (verses 20-23).

Pharaoh's Dream

Scholars have debated endlessly when Joseph lived. Many have suggested it might have been during the Hyksos period of Egyptian history (1750-1550 B.C.), when Asiatics rather than native Egyptians ruled the northern part of the country.[32] These Asiatics, who had gradually migrated into the lush delta and Nile River valley during a period of several centuries, assimilated to Egyptian culture and then seized political control. If Joseph was brought to Egypt during this period, the fact that the king or pharaoh shared similar ethnic backgrounds may have encouraged him to trust in the Hebrew slave. As God worked out events for the future survival of Joseph and his family He did what He has constantly done in human history—He used specific human beings and human circumstances to accomplish His purposes. Because of the human mask God so often wears, His people, as in the case of Joseph himself, usually do not see His guidance and providence until He has completed His plans. An observer in Pharaoh's court may have concluded that the king favored Joseph because of their common cultural ties—fellow Asiatics in a foreign land. But the king did not have to appoint Joseph second in command or even listen to his interpretation of the dreams. The Holy Spirit works through the familiar things of life. Only later will God open the eyes of faith so that people can see the marvelous things He has done.

The members of Pharaoh's court would have understood much of what happened. People in their world believed that the gods communicated to human beings through dreams. If it was a really important message to a ruler, the gods might emphasize that fact by sending a double dream.[33] The only thing unusual about the present experience was that the king needed help to interpret the dream.[34] Since the Egyptian king was considered a god himself, he was expected to understand the divine messages. But here he asked for help from others. The Hebrew word that Genesis uses to describe the specialists Pharaoh sent for comes from a technical Egyptian term that some scholars believe refers to dream interpreters. A second century B.C. inscription applied it to the court official Imhotep as he advised a pharaoh about an impending seven-year famine.[35]

Even Pharaoh's dreams employed familiar imagery. Cattle and stalks of grain were a part of everyday life. The cow was also the visible form of one of Egypt's major deities, the goddess Hathor. Famines frequently afflicted the ancient world, even in Egypt with its normally reliable source of irrigation, the river Nile. Although the annual flooding of the Nile's valley made Egypt more secure than most of the Middle East, changes in the rainfall patterns over the mountains of Ethiopia, the Nile's source, could seriously affect the people of the valley. Too much as well as too little water could trigger a famine. If the river level fell too low, it would not spread over the land and fill the vital irrigation canals. Too much would prevent the farmers from being able to plant their crops at the right time.

People in the ancient world barely survived from one harvest to the next. Anything that destroyed or reduced a crop's yield could plunge a whole society into disaster. While Egypt could grow up to three crops a year and produced more of a surplus than most ancient lands, even it was vulnerable. Although they usually portrayed only idealistic scenes, Egyptian artists did occasionally acknowledge the precariousness of life by depicting emaciated famine victims on the walls of tombs and public buildings. The Egyptian *Visions of Neferti,* dating to the reign of Amenemhet I (1991-1962 B.C.), described a vision foretelling such a famine.[36]

The famine that struck the ancient Near East in Joseph's time was not out of the ordinary. As Derek Kidner observes, Joseph does not describe the approaching famine as a judgment against Egypt or call for repentance. Rather it was "one of life's irregularities"[37] that God chose to employ for His own purposes. God daily works through the humdrum of each of our lives. We need to let Him open our eyes to see His providence in the mundane things of life. If we do not learn to recognize God in the world of the ordinary, we will fail to see Him even in the miraculous.

After describing the looming crisis, Joseph outlined a plan for dealing with it. He suggested that Pharaoh select a capable leader and make him head of a program to store food during the predicted seven good harvests to have when the seven bad years came (Gen. 41:25-36). The Egyptian king liked Joseph's proposal so well that he decided to put him in charge of it (verses 37-40). Like Potiphar and the chief jailer, Pharaoh recognized that God was with Joseph (verses 38, 39). He too would place all that he had in Joseph's hand. The imprisoned slave had suddenly become second in command of the mighty Egyptian Empire.

---

[1] See, for example, Bruce J. Malina and Richard L. Rohrbaugh, *Social Science Commentary on the Synoptic Gospels* (Minneapolis: Fortress Press, 1992), in their comments on honor and shame. Although they focus on the New Testament period, the issue of honor and shame has existed throughout the history of the Mediterranean world, and still

survives as a fundamental strand of the social fabric there even today.

[2] J. H. Walton and V. H. Matthews, *The IVP Bible Background Commentary: Genesis-Deuteronomy,* p. 70. Many introductory books on the Old Testament have reproductions of the Beni-hasan tomb murals.

[3] W. Brueggeman, *Genesis,* p. 300.

[4] *HarperCollins Bible Commentary,* p. 112.

[5] *Ibid.*

[6] Walton and Matthews, p. 70.

[7] Notice that dreams come in pairs in the Joseph story.

[8] Jacob believes the symbols of the sun and moon to be him and one of his wives. Derek Kidner considers "your mother" as referring to Leah, it being "unrealistic to make it imply that Rachel was still alive" (*Genesis,* p. 181).

[9] Apparently not every aspect of it comes true. Scripture never depicts Jacob's parents bowing before him.

[10] Kidner, p. 181.

[11] John Sanders, *The God Who Risks: A Theology of Providence* (Downers Grove, Ill.: InterVarsity Press, 1998), p. 75.

[12] The fact that Joseph was still at the home encampment is another indication of his father's favoritism toward Rachel's firstborn. Jacob wanted to keep the young man near him.

[13] For biblical examples of laws governing grazing rights, see Exodus 22:5. Cf. Law 57 of the much more ancient Code of Hammurabi.

[14] Victor H. Matthews, *Manners and Customs in the Bible* (Peabody, Mass.: Hendrickson Publishers, 1988), pp. 9, 10.

[15] Walton and Matthews, p. 48.

[16] *The IVP Women's Bible Commentary,* p. 25.

[17] *New Dictionary of Biblical Theology,* ed. T. Desmond Alexander and Brian S. Rosner (Leicester, Eng.: InterVarsity Press, 2000), p. 742.

[18] J. Fokkelman, *Reading Biblical Narrative,* p. 81.

[19] Victor P. Hamilton, *Handbook of the Pentateuch.* 2nd ed. (Grand Rapids: Baker Academic, 2005), p. 129.

[20] The word "bless" and the theme of blessing frequently appear in the Joseph story.

[21] Here again we see the biblical love of bringing out patterns and parallels, sometimes with a twist. In the case of the patriarchs Abraham and Isaac, foreign rulers had wanted their wives. Now, in an ironic variation of the pattern, we see the wife of a foreign "ruler" seeking the patriarch himself.

[22] Joyce Tyldesley, *Daughters of Isis: Women of Ancient Egypt* (London: Penguin Books, 1995), pp. 60-62.

[23] Jacob wore Esau's clothing as well as animal skins on his arms to trick his father (Gen. 27). Tamar kept Jacob's signet seal that he wore on a cord (Gen. 38). And first Joseph's robe almost caused his death—then his tunic compromised him.

[24] T. Longman III, *How to Read Genesis,* p. 153.

[25] C. Meyers, "The Family in Early Israel," p. 26.

[26] *Ibid.*

[27] Tyldesley, pp. 82, 122, 123.

[28] *Ibid.,* p. 82.

[29] Walton and Matthews, p. 74.

[30] Egyptians believed that only experts could interpret dreams. Unfortunately, they would not readily be available in a prison.

[31] Notice that Joseph here regards Canaan as the land of his own people—"the land of the Hebrews" (Gen. 40:15).

[32] See Jack Finegan, *Handbook of Biblical Chronology: Principles of Time Reckoning in the Ancient World and Problems of Chronology in the Bible,* rev. ed. (Peabody, Mass.: Hendrickson Publishers, 1998), pp. 207-224.

[33] Walton and Matthews, p. 75.

[34] *Ibid.*

[35] *Ibid.*

[36] *Ibid.*

[37] Kidner, p. 196.

13

A Family Restored

Genesis 41:41-50:26

After Pharaoh announced that he had put Joseph over all Egypt, he presented him with various insignia of his new office: a signet ring, a gold chain, and special linen garments (Gen. 41:41, 42). Ancient Egyptian paintings often depict these symbols of power. Joseph's brothers had stripped him of his special coat and thrown him down into a pit. But the king dressed him in fine linen and elevated him to the second-highest position in the land. As an immature lad Joseph had dreamed of others bowing to him. Now he watched as the nobility of Egypt bent the knee to him. Pharaoh also gave him a wife, Asenath, daughter of Potiphera, priest of On. The marriage allied him with one of the most powerful priestly families in ancient Egypt.[1]

Joseph put his plan for national survival into operation, and when the famine struck, Egypt was ready (verses 46-49, 53, 54). As crops failed in surrounding lands, word spread to them that Egypt still had food. The narrator declared that "all the world came to Joseph in Egypt to buy grain" (verse 57). Although it may have been only the ancient Near East involved, the biblical author emphasized "all the world" to recall the theme of God blessing the nations through Joseph, one of the offspring of Abraham.

Among those who came to purchase food were 10 of Joseph's brothers (Gen. 42:1-3). They would comprise a large enough caravan to handle both the needed pack animals and to discourage attacks from bandits. But Jacob refused to allow Benjamin to accompany them (verse 4). He had lost one of Rachel's two children, and he wanted nothing to happen to the remaining one.

A Family Restored

Joseph had announced after the birth of his first child that the Lord had enabled him to forget his father's house. But that was not to be. Having complete control of the grain reserves, he must have often personally supervised its sale. At least he was present when the brothers arrived. We can only imagine what conflicting emotions must have raced through his mind at the sight of them. Because he had grown older, dressed like an Egyptian, and wore the heavy kohl eye shadow used by both men and women to protect their eyes, they did not recognize him. Besides, Joseph would have been the last person they would have ever expected to encounter.

As Joseph studied them, suddenly those dreams of long ago flashed into his mind—dreams that had caused his brothers to sell him into the slavery that had led him to Egypt. Eleven brothers had bowed to him in them, but only 10 were here. And where were his parents? Could something have happened to them? He had to find out—and he would do it in his own way. In that moment he knew what he must do.

Glaring at them, he declared, "You are spies; you have come to see the nakedness of the land!" (verse 9). The people of the surrounding nations were always trying to infiltrate the fertile Nile delta. The Egyptians had constructed a chain of forts out in the desert along the eastern edge of the delta to control the flow of people into the land, but they could not stop everyone.

In their defense the brothers explained that they were 10 members of a family that had once included 12 sons, and that one brother was now no more (verse 13). Why would they mention such a detail? The fact that they alluded to Joseph might suggest that God was working on their hearts and minds in preparation for their eventual reunion with the brother they had abandoned to slavery.

Joseph decided to test, in a way that echoed what had happened so many years before, what kind of men they now were. He demanded a hostage. The rest would once again have to return home and explain to their father why a brother was missing. While Joseph would allow them to buy food this time, he told them, they would not get any more unless they returned with the youngest brother (verses 18-20).

"Alas, we are paying the penalty for what we did to our brother," they told each other, an admission surely prompted by the Holy Spirit. Time had not dimmed the memory of what they had done. Divine power had only intensified it. Now they could feel emotions that would have been impossible years before. "We saw his anguish when he pleaded with us, but we would not listen. That is why this anguish has come upon us" (verse 21).

Reuben reminded them that he had protested what they had done (verse 22). None of them wondered about an Egyptian official's strange interest in their family. They were caught up in their collective guilt. Joseph chose Simeon as the hostage[2] and sent the brothers on their way after he had secretly placed in their grain sacks the money they had spent for the food.

When the brothers reached Canaan, they did have to explain—as Joseph had intended—why Simeon had not returned with them. It plunged them back into the emotions they had gone through after they had sold their brother into slavery. Perhaps they also realized that they had in a very real sense traded Simeon for food. Then when they began emptying the grain sacks, the bars and rings of silver they had used to pay for the food came tumbling out with the wheat. Could Jacob have concluded that his sons had actually sold Simeon for that food? A hint of his suspicion may appear in his comment "I am the one you have bereaved of children: Joseph is no more, and Simeon is no more" (verse 36). In response to their report that the Egyptian official would not sell them any more food unless their youngest brother accompanied them, their father snapped, "And now you would take Benjamin."[3] Reuben offered his two sons as hostages and was even willing to forfeit their lives if anything happened to Benjamin (verse 37), but Jacob was adamant that his youngest son would not go (verse 38). The journey would lead only to more sorrow for him—by implication, another death. Once again Reuben found himself frustrated in another attempt to protect one of Rachel's sons.

But the famine was relentless. Jacob's family could not survive much longer. He had no choice but to send his sons back for more food.[4] That meant that Benjamin would have to go with them. As with Abraham and his son, Isaac, Jacob must first lose Benjamin to save him. He must trust God. "May God Almighty grant you mercy before the man" (Gen. 43:14).[5] But as when he had feared the reunion with Esau, his faith was still weak. Jacob had sent presents to his brother, hoping to curry his favor. Now he again tried the same ploy (verse 11). The brothers carried with them the same items as had the caravan that took Joseph into Egypt—as well as the other son of Rachel (Gen. 37:25; Gen. 43:11). They left for Egypt with their father's bitter words echoing in their ears: "If I am bereaved of my children, I am bereaved" (Gen. 43:14).

After their arrival in Egypt, Joseph ordered them taken to his private residence, a turn of events that frightened them. The servant did not tell them that it was for a meal, and they assumed that Joseph was having them punished, perhaps enslaved, because of the money that they had found in their grain sacks (verses 16-18). When they explained to the steward that they had brought the money back, he assured them that he had already received their money. And the steward echoed a major theme of Genesis: God's intervention in human affairs (verse 23).

After Joseph appeared at his residence, the brothers bowed and gave him the presents they had brought. They still did not question his curiosity about their family. The sight of Benjamin overwhelmed Joseph, and he had to leave the room (verse 30). Regaining his self-control, he returned and ordered the meal served. The fact that he had the brothers seated by age puzzled them, but they made no reference to it (verse 33).

Joseph supplied the men the food they had come for—but he had one final test for them. For once and for all he would see what kind of individuals they had perhaps become since they had sold him into slavery. He instructed his steward to plant Joseph's special silver cup[6] in Benjamin's sack. Then, after the brothers had left the city, Joseph told the steward to pursue them and accuse them of stealing the diviner's cup (Gen. 44:1-5), which he did.

The charge shocked the brothers. Why would they do such a thing? they asked. Reflecting Jacob's response to Laban's accusation of stealing the *teraphim,* they replied that if the steward found the cup on anyone, that person would die and the rest would become slaves (verses 6-9). The steward accepted the challenge, modifying the sentence from death to slavery for the actual thief and freedom for the rest (verse 10). He searched each brother's sack, beginning with the oldest brother and concluding with Benjamin. Overcome with horror as they saw the cup in the youngest brother's sack, they tore their clothes in grief, just as their father had done after Joseph's disappearance.

Back at Joseph's house, the brothers threw themselves on the ground before him (verse 14). When Joseph demanded, "What deed is this that you have done?" (verse 15), Judah seemed to respond to something more than just the allegation of stealing the cup. "God has found out the guilt of your servants" (verse 16). Could it have been a confession of all the guilt they had borne for so many years?

Joseph stated that he would allow the others to return home to their father. He would claim only Benjamin as a slave (verse 17). But Judah, who had suggested that they sell Joseph into slavery, now pleaded for Benjamin's release from slavery (verses 18-34). If Jacob lost the last son of his beloved Rachel, he explained, it would cause his death (verses 30-34). Judah then offered himself as substitute for Benjamin (verse 33).[7] The brothers are willing to sacrifice themselves for one of Rachel's sons, something they would not have done years before.

As Joseph had listened to them struggle to make sense of the frightening situations he had plunged them into, he desperately wanted to believe what he witnessed. But he had been hurt deeply. He too needed healing. God also worked to remove the pain of betrayal and abandonment in his heart. As the brothers had grown to sense their need for forgiveness, Joseph also realized his own need to give such forgiveness. Forgiveness was the key to all their healing. But forgiveness may take time both to receive and to give. Joseph had spent much time making sure that his brothers had changed. And it would be just as hard for them to accept.

Finally, unable to control his emotions any longer, Joseph sent his servants away and revealed his identity to his brothers, asking if Jacob was still alive.[8] Stunned, the brothers couldn't say anything. Their terror increased when he added. "I am your brother, Joseph, whom you sold into Egypt" (Gen. 45:4). Fully aware of how they must feel, he told them not to be distressed or angry with themselves because that had sent him into Egyptian slavery. Finding forgiveness from others must also including forgiving one's self.

God had used what had happened as a way of preserving their family, Joseph explained (verses 5-8). The Lord could take even the deliberately torn fabric of life and reweave it to accomplish His will, thus bringing good out of evil and disaster. A central theme of Genesis—and all Scripture—is God's unending desire to deliver and save. That deliverance involves restoration in its infinite forms. Joseph immediate declared his intention of reuniting the family. He ordered his brothers to hurry back to Jacob, tell him that his lost son was alive, and bring the rest of the family to Egypt. Once they returned to Egypt, Joseph would care for all of them so that the famine would not destroy them (verses 9-11).

Jacob came to Egypt, and Pharaoh honored him. The years passed, and after a long life, the patriarch realized that his death was approaching. He made Joseph promise that he would not bury him in Egypt. Then the father offered his final blessings. First he called Joseph and blessed and adopted the two sons by Asenath (Gen. 48).[9] Finally Jacob summoned the rest of his sons.[10]

Jacob Blesses His Sons

A father's final blessing to his children was not something to be taken lightly. "So significant were deathbed utterances that a literary form evolved early in ancient Israel governing the character of testaments. A patriarch's final wishes established destinies. His sons and daughters waited anxiously for the paternal blessing, and implemented it by word and deed. The occasion of the dying word was solemn, one could even say sacred. For it was then that a father voiced his most precious wish for his children."

As Jacob presented his deathbed prophecy he shifted into poetry. Biblical poetry is lyrical and emotional, experiencing the feelings of the moment rather than narrating or just giving information. The patriarch also indulged into extensive wordplays that cannot be captured in translation. The Hebrew of "Dan shall judge" in Genesis 49:16, for example, is *dan yadin,* and the original of "Gad shall be raided by raiders" (verse 19) is *gad gedud yegudennu.* Space permits only a few brief observations about the prophetic poem. First, Reuben, the firstborn, has lost his position as leader of the brothers because of his affair with his stepmother Bilhah (Gen. 35:22). Second, Judah has assumed the most prominent role among the 12 brothers. Jacob predicted that his offspring would have dominion among the other tribes (Gen. 49:8-12). His poem has more verses for Judah (verses 8-12)[12] and Joseph (verses 22-26) than the other sons. Their tribes will have the greatest role to play once Israel has settled Canaan.

And third, the section on Simeon and Levi is especially interesting in that it offers an example of how human choice can alter even prophecy. Jacob presents a rather negative image of them because of their involvement in the slaughter of the people of Shechem (verses 5-7; cf. Gen. 34). Moses' counterpart to Jacob's deathbed blessing (Deut. 33) depicts the tribe descended from Levi in a much more positive light (verses 8-12) because of their response to a tragic situation during the wilderness wandering (Ex. 32). While the tribe of Simeon virtually disappears, that of Levi assumes a prominent role in Israel. Prophecy is conditional. People can choose how they will respond to it and thus alter its outcome.

But the most important aspect of the deathbed testament was that God would bring into reality the blessing promised Abraham through the offspring of Jacob's sons. A vital part of it is the divine future rescue of His people "in days to come" (Gen. 49:1; cf. Num. 24:14-24; Deut. 31:24) so that they may fulfill their mission to bless all the nations. Genesis 49 closes by employing the word "blessing" three times (verse 28), drawing the reader's attention back to the theme of blessing woven through the book from Genesis 1:28 on.

Jacob's Death and Burial

Jacob repeated to all his sons that he did not want to be buried in Egypt. He instructed them to take his body to the cave of Machpelah (Gen. 49:29-32), that token of the future Promised Land that Abraham had bought long before. His burial there would be his own affirmation of God's promises to his ancestors. And with that request, he breathed his last (verse 33).

The Egyptians traditionally spent 70 days embalming a body, drying it with a natural salt known as natron and then wrapping it in linen bandages. Genesis 50:3 states that the embalmers finished Jacob's body in 40 days.[13] The funeral procession carrying Jacob's body from Egypt to Canaan foreshadowed the Exodus. By following the eastern side of the Dead Sea and entering Canaan from the east, it even mirrored the route of the future Israelites. A large delegation of Egyptians accompanied Jacob's family.[14]

Even now the brothers still found it hard to accept that Joseph had really forgiven them. With the influence of their father gone, would the spirit of revenge burst into flame in their younger brother's heart? They came to him as a group and told him that "your father" had instructed them to ask Joseph to forgive them for what they had done (verse 16).[15] Perhaps they feared that only Joseph's love for their father had prompted him not to seek revenge, and now Jacob was dead. The request reduced Joseph to tears.[16] His grief must have intensified even more when they threw themselves down before him and announced, "We are here as your slaves" (verse 18). It was not the way he had so long ago visualized them as bowing to him.

After telling them not to be afraid, he repeated what he had told them so many years before—that God had used the evil they had intended as a vehicle to preserve them. As for now, Joseph would continue to provide for them (verses 19-21).

Joseph's declaration that God is control of history is not a new theme in Genesis. The book has dealt with the concept from its beginning. Turner observes that believers have long puzzled over how to relate God's sovereignty with human free will. "Both divine sovereignty (e.g., Ex. 9:12; Rom. 8:29, 30) and human free will (e.g., Joshua 25:15; John 7:17) are affirmed in Scripture. But how can both be true? For if God is absolutely sovereign, then we are not free. And if we are absolutely free, then God is not sovereign. The Bible does not provide a solution to this problem. Rather, it presents the issue as a paradox, that is, the contradiction is only apparent, not real. If we wish to see examples of how we are free to choose our own destiny, then we can read the narratives [of Genesis] and see Adam, Eve, Cain, Lamech, Abraham and the rest do just that. But if all we had was human free will, we would be in a real dilemma. The genealogies of Genesis 1-11 remind us of the other side of the equation. Through their repetitions and predictability they witness to God's leading in human history. They show that life is not merely a random collection of events driven by human free will. There is meaning in life. In other words: God is sovereign."[17]

The story of Joseph began with a broken and estranged family. He had been an immature young man with a sense of destiny but far from ready to fulfill it. The older brothers had been violent and deceitful, true sons of their father, Jacob. Angry and frustrated by what their father had done to them, they had given in to their hatred and had avenged themselves on their father through the son he had loved too unwisely. But God had been using both the ordinary and the extraordinary to transform them to the point that they could weep together.

What had seemed at first only cruel and meaningless events had become in the weaving of God a way to mature Joseph into a powerful leader who saved not only his family but also the whole nation of Egypt and many from the surrounding lands. That did not mean that the Lord had intended the brothers to abuse Joseph and sell him into slavery. The Lord sets the goal; then He may let human beings choose the means, whether for good or bad. But even if they opt for evil, He can still bring good out of it.

What the Lord did in Jacob's family He longs to do for all His children. We all need healing before we can live as a family for eternity. And we all must be transformed before we can be a blessing for the nations.

The book of Genesis ends with Joseph in a mummy case (Gen. 50:26). The ancient Egyptians believed that the body occupied its coffin even in the afterlife. But the God of Abraham, Isaac, and Jacob promises to raise His children from their graves, and they will live an eternal existence far beyond what the people of the valley of the Nile could ever imagine.

---

[1] Interestingly, the name of Asenath's father, Potiphera, is just another form of Potiphar.

[2] Could Joseph have selected Simeon because of his leadership in the slaughter at Shechem? And is Levi not mentioned because of the rehabilitation of his descendants when they defended Moses during the revolt in the wilderness? Other commentators suggest that Joseph chose Simeon because he was Leah's second son and thus would be held until Rachel's second son came.

[3] In their report of their encounter with Joseph they do not mention their imprison-

ment and the death threat.

[4] The gruff way Jacob speaks to the brothers contrasts with the protectiveness he shows toward Benjamin.

[5] An allusion to another man, the one he wrestled at the Jabbok.

[6] Since Egypt had no silver deposits, it was more valuable than gold. The cup also seemed to have some special significance.

[7] Judah's speech, the longest of any in Genesis 37-50, moves Joseph to tears and convinces him to shed his disguise and reveal himself to his perplexed brothers. Chapters 37, 38, and 42-45 all employ clothing and various forms of disguise. People both recognize and are deceived by what someone has worn. The brother ties his speech together with such imagery as that of master/servant and references to "face."

[8] The ancient listener to the Joseph story would have seen his reaction here as an ideal demonstration of sibling affection.

[9] Jacob's blessing of the younger son, Ephraim, echoes his blessing even though he was the younger son.

[10] This section parallels in topic and arrangement of material two other sections of Genesis: Genesis 22:15-25:10 and 35:9-29. See *Eerdmans Commentary on the Bible,* pp. 62, 70. It shows the intricately linked structure of the biblical book.

[11] J. L. Crenshaw, *Samson,* p. 27.

[12] Moses has much less to say about Judah (Deut. 33:7). Instead, he gives Levi the greatest blessing of all (verses 8-12) because of intervening events (Ex. 32:25-29).

[13] Interestingly, various experiments have shown that extending mummification beyond 40 days will not increase its effectiveness (Fergus Fleming, *The Way to Eternity: Egyptian Myth* [New York: Barnes and Noble, 2003], p. 98).

[14] Perhaps echoing the later "mixed multitude" (Ex. 12:38, KJV) of the Exodus.

[15] The narrator does not indicate whether Jacob had said such a thing or whether the brothers had invented it. Some commentators see it as the final act of deceit and duplicity in Genesis.

[16] It is the first time that Scripture records them asking him for forgiveness.

[17] L. Turner, *Back to the Present,* pp. 74, 75.